IMAGES
of America

NOLENSVILLE

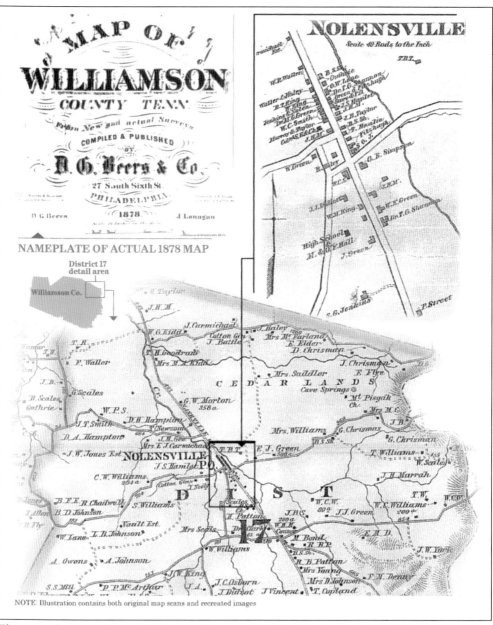

This map shows northeast Williamson County in 1878, with inset detail of Nolensville at top right. (Illustration by Kent Travis, original map courtesy of Heritage Foundation of Williamson County.)

On the Cover: The Nolensville Co-Operative Creamery was formed in 1921 by more than 200 dairy farmers whose purpose was to make premium butter. Owned and controlled by the farmers, it was quickly profitable. The creamery, which won contests for its butter, operated until 1957. ¬he building, part of Nolensville's historic district, has been repurposed as shops over the years. ¬rtesy of Williamson County Archives.)

IMAGES
of America

NOLENSVILLE

Beth Lothers and Vicky Travis

ARCADIA
PUBLISHING

Published by Arcadia Publishing
Charleston, South Carolina

Printed in the United States of America

Library of Congress Control Number: 2018931064

For all general information, please contact Arcadia Publishing:
Telephone 843-853-2070
Fax 843-853-0044
E-mail sales@arcadiapublishing.com
For customer service and orders:
Toll-Free 1-888-313-2665

Visit us on the Internet at www.arcadiapublishing.com

Dedicated to Evelyn Gillespie Hyde Bennett (1927–2018).
Newer to Nolensville like us, she spent the last years of her
purpose-driven and graceful life loving and preserving our town.

CONTENTS

ACKNOWLEDGMENTS

We stand on the shoulders of amazing, generous town historians who have come before us. The book *Nolensville: 1797–1987*, locally referred to as the "Red Book," was a massive undertaking by Peggy Stephenson Wilson and her team in the age of nondigital production to tell Nolensville's story. The Nolensville Historical Society (NHS) published six historical journals, with the time-intensive research of historian Marie Williams Batey, that have been invaluable resources for us. Our intent is not to repeat these publications but to add to our knowledge in this image-based work and make Nolensville's history accessible for visitors, newcomers, and even longtime Nolensvillians.

Thank you to the Heritage Foundation of Williamson County's Rick Warwick, the master county historian. Thank you to Carroll Moore, Michelle Jenkins, and Juli King at NHS and artist John Strasser for his illustrations. Thank you to Mayor Jimmy Alexander for lending us his Red Book. Special thanks to our families for their help and support. Beth thanks husband Ted, daughter Corinne, and son Jacob. Vicky thanks husband Kent, daughter Sophie, and son Jacob.

We've been blessed to meet with many families and individuals, who often let us spend hours in their homes scanning their precious photographs. Their stories have been inspiring, funny, and sometimes tough. We love and appreciate each one of you. Some of the storied past of Nolensville does not have a photograph to reflect it, and some photographs are truly worth a thousand words. We hope people see themselves in the photographs of others in the bigger story of a community.

Abbreviations used in the book include:

TSLA	Tennessee State Library and Archives
Heritage Foundation	Heritage Foundation of Williamson County
Nolensville Historic School	Nolensville Historic School and Museum
NFUMC	Nolensville First United Methodist Church

INTRODUCTION

The collective hands that axed and carved through the wilderness cleared the way for more settlers to come to what was the western frontier. Large migrations from North Carolina routed by wagon through the mountains to eventually settle along Mill Creek. Whether they were staking a claim to a land grant received through service in the Revolutionary War or they purchased a portion from the original recipients, and whether they came as family or slaves, the early settlers made their home in what would be known as Nolensville within territory established in 1796 as the state of Tennessee.

The first inhabitants of Nolensville left behind prehistoric fragments along Mill Creek. The first explorers in the area arrived in 1500 to find abandoned village sites. It is not known if the Native Americans migrated to other parts of North America or disappeared from disease or war. In the late 1700s, European American settlers most likely encountered hunter-and-gatherer members of the Cherokee and Chickasaw tribes defending their hunting grounds. Log homes were built with openings to allow settlers to fire upon raiders. Attacks on settlers had lessened by around 1800, and numerous migrations to the Nolensville area began from North Carolina, South Carolina, and Virginia, with the largest from Rockingham County, North Carolina.

Nolensville derives its name from William Nolen, a Revolutionary War veteran from Virginia who owned the land that became the commercial village. Legend has it that in 1797, while traveling along Mill Creek just south of Nashville, Nolen experienced a broken wagon wheel. Repairing the wheel required wood to be cut and seasoned, and pieces to be made by hand. The providential pause made him search no further, with the immediate availability of land, wild game, and water. Nolen's stopping place became his homeplace, and the broken wheel serves as the town symbol to this day.

Some evidence suggests that Delilah Cantrell of North Carolina was William Nolen's first wife and mother to his first seven children. Family historians assert that Delilah passed away in October 1800 in Williamson County. In 1801, Nolen married Sarah Cantrell, a cousin of his first wife, and they had nine more children together in Nolensville. Several accounts reveal that the Nolen children wore bells around their necks to prevent them from getting lost beyond the clearing or taken by Native Americans.

Williamson County, in which Nolensville is situated, was established by the Tennessee General Assembly on October 26, 1799, and named in honor of Dr. Hugh Williamson, lawmaker and surgeon general of North Carolina during the Revolutionary War. With the major migrations to Tennessee came tremendous growth. The county population in 1800 was in the hundreds, and by 1810 it was 13,000. Families who contributed to the development of the Nolensville area lived beyond town boundaries in what is considered southern Davidson County as well as northwestern Rutherford County.

Children and grandchildren of Revolutionary War patriots, Nolensville residents took hold of the opportunity presented, and by 1820, Nolensville became the commercial center of northeastern

Williamson County. There were hotels, livery stables, stores, mills, blacksmith shops, office buildings, and every type of craftsman available, including saddle and harness makers, cabinet and wagon makers, and even boat and cigar ("sigar") makers. One of the earliest physicians in Williamson County came from the Nolensville area. Dr. Solomon Humphreys left behind seven medical books and assorted medicines when he died in 1817. Experienced midwives also assisted women during the life-threatening process of childbirth.

In comparison with large plantations around the South, Nolensville farms were smaller, with fewer slaves in the agricultural economy. It was common for migrating families to bring slaves with them to settle the land. In 1820, some of the larger slave owners in Nolensville had six to twenty-eight slaves, depending on the amount of land they owned. As it was for the Native Americans who taught the settlers how to grow it, corn was an essential crop. Cotton, wheat, and tobacco were also favored crops, and many settlers also raised cattle. Waller Chapel marks the location of the first cotton gin. Nolensville would come to be known for dairy and butter making through its Co-Op Creamery. The historic creamery building and the Nolensville Feed Mill have been utilized as retail and food venues.

What was originally a Native American trail became a rough wagon road, stagecoach route, and in 1838, the Nolensville Turnpike. Originally 15 miles long from Nashville to Nolensville, the toll road was eventually extended to Triune. Toll houses collected fees every five miles and provided funds for road maintenance prior to the paving of Nolensville Road in 1929. The long state highway that bears the Nolensville name stretches from Fourth Avenue in Nashville south through the town of Nolensville in Williamson County. The road, bordered on one side by Mill Creek and on the other by a tributary, affords a narrow strip of land where William Nolen's property was situated and where commercial lots developed into what is Nolensville's historic district, the heart of the town.

On January 20, 1838, a city charter for Nolensville was approved by the State of Tennessee. State-appointed commissioners were charged to "lay off and mark the limits of the town of Nolensville in the county of Williamson and make out a plan and plat of the same." Commissioners included Samuel Bittix (or Bittick), James Green, John Hay, Littlebury Johnson, R.D. Maury (or Murray), and John Nolen. With no record of a functioning government, the charter was repealed on March 2, 1885, by the state. The county commission represented Nolensville until it was incorporated in 1996 as a municipality.

This image-based work provides a glimpse of the stamina and innovation it took to not only survive but also create commerce, places of education and worship, purposeful organizations, and recreation. Natural disasters such as tornados and floods were as threatening as the frequent fires that turned landmark structures to ash. The Civil War challenged local existence, both for those leaving to serve and for those left behind to maintain family life and endure early Union occupation. Loss of life and property was not afforded an ample grieving period before the challenges of Reconstruction required the community's complete attention. Freedom from slavery and the surname of a former owner did not provide an easy path for African Americans who for the first time could choose for themselves, as the first white settlers did before them, whether or not Nolensville would remain their home.

New Nolensvillians would come to reside as spouses, teachers, or laborers. Some would again realize the loss of what they had gained through the Great Depression. Some would leave to fight wars in distant lands, and some would return only to be mourned. Integration would bring schools, sports, and businesses to reflect the intertwined community spirit that pockets of Nolensville already reflected with neighbors helping neighbors.

The hand that toiled and struck at the rocky soil had a fingerprint unique in all the world. No man, woman, or child could be exactly like another, nor could Nolensville be like any other Southern town. Nolensville is as rare as the individual fingerprints that created it. Nolensville has a fingerprint all its own. Its early settlers came to a wild natural canvas on which they would paint their stories and their dreams.

One

SETTLER STORIES

After the Revolutionary War, the state of North Carolina was cash poor but had an abundance of land in its western frontier—the land that would become Tennessee. In 1783, North Carolina began issuing land grants to recipients who fought in the war, served as land surveyors for the state, or performed some other function the state deemed worthy. The number of acres was often tied to rank, but the basic size was 640 acres. The recipients ventured out to locate the undeveloped land they would title. Some patriots were already established on existing property and chose to subdivide and sell their grant to would-be settlers.

Nashville settlers with the Donelson or Robertson groups in 1779 and 1780 had not received the land promised them. Therefore, the North Carolina legislature enacted a preemption law in 1780 that awarded land ownership to settlers who improved property occupied with a structure. Some land grants were also awarded to family members of those killed by Native American raids at Fort Nashboro. Signers of the Cumberland Compact who settled in Nolensville included Henry Guthrie, Thomas Shannon, and David Maxwell.

Those migrating to what would become Tennessee in 1796 traveled mainly by wagon train through the mountains of North Carolina and Cumberland Gap. The grit required for the journey foretold the resilience the wild lands would require of them. Recognizable Nolensville families from early migrations are evident in the names of local roads and developments.

Some settlers already had means, and their initial log structures would become grander. Others came with very little and set their sights on the opportunity of working and living off their own land. There are tales of those interested in leaving something behind like a domineering patriarch or unrequited love, as well as stories of those striking out toward the hopeful unknown. Children followed their families. Slaves followed their owners. The betrothed followed their husbands. Those who came created not only the tapestry of their future but also the future of what would become a bustling town. Every family that came has their story, and these are but a few.

William Nolen (1760–1850) was born in Virginia. Having served in the Revolutionary War, he was granted land and came to Tennessee in about 1797. Legend has it that a broken wagon wheel landed him along Mill Creek, and the area's natural resources influenced him to stake his claim on the 120 acres that would later bear his name. Nolen purchased additional land and marked off lots on the original plan of Nolensville in 1818. He owned an ordinary, a tavern that served food and also operated as an inn. (Courtesy of Rev. Alfred and Evelyn Bennett.)

Originally from North Carolina, Sarah Cantrell Nolen (c. 1776–1859) bore nine children to William Nolen in Nolensville. Sarah raised 16 children in all, including William's first seven children by his first wife, Sarah's cousin Delilah Cantrell Nolen (1761–1800). The Nolens built their log cabin along the creek in the northwest portion of what is the historic district and are believed to be buried on the original property. (Courtesy of Rev. Alfred and Evelyn Bennett.)

After the Nolen home site changed owners through the years, it was purchased by Newt McCord. McCord served as a Williamson County commissioner for 43 years, raised his family on the historic site, and farmed Roseland Farms, northeast of town on Nolensville Road. When the house was to be torn down in 2009, Rev. Alfred Bennett and Evelyn Gillespie Hyde Bennett moved the McCord home to their adjacent property in the historic district on Nolensville Road and uncovered the pictured log structure of William Nolen's cabin within. The rocks between the logs typify cabin construction of the period. Portraits of William and Sarah Nolen hang on the wall of this restored home (below). Some of the original logs from the William Nolen cabin are displayed through a glass divider. (Above, courtesy of Rev. Alfred and Evelyn Bennett; below, courtesy of Vicky Travis.)

Sherwood Green (1766–1840) traveled to Tennessee by oxcart when the area was still part of North Carolina. A land surveyor for the US government, he was often paid with land grants. By 1830, Green had amassed an estate of 1,130 acres. He settled where the home stands on Rocky Fork Road and came with his friends, the Nolen and Col. William Christmas families. He married his first wife, Martha Christmas (1784–1828), in 1800, and she bore 11 children. After her death, Green married his neighbor's daughter Mary Ozburn Johnson (1802–1853) in 1829. Their son Edward J. Green (1830–1901) is pictured at left and above with his wife, Mary Louise King (1837–1922), and three of their eight children. A daughter of Benjamin Tarver and Susan Matthew King, Mary Louise, married Edward in 1852 at Nolensville's King's Inn. (Both, courtesy of Janice Page Green.)

John William "J.W." Williams (1848–1940), a Nolensville native and the son of Clement Williams (1814–1896) and Tabitha Barnes (died 1853), was a large landowner in the late 1800s and early 1900s. He married Susan Owen (1852–1874) and had two children. After she died, he married Louise Osburn, with whom he had 11 more children. Williams owned most of the land on either side of Clovercroft Road from Bittick's Creek to the historic district. He owned several stores with his sons, was one of the founders of the Bank of Nolensville, and helped build Nolensville First United Methodist Church (then Mount Olivet). He bought and ran the King Hotel (formerly the King's Inn) and livery in 1881. (Courtesy of Larry Williams.)

Living to be 91, J.W. Williams imprinted Nolensville in significant ways. In his older years, he would visit son B.O. Williams's store to sit on its porch, which was a community gathering place. (Courtesy of Carrie Stephenson Ozburn.)

The Gooch home was across from the Nolensville First United Methodist Church. British descendants, the Gooches came from a prominent Virginia family and followed the North Carolina migration pattern. The Williamson County ancestors of the Nolensville Gooch family were William and Frances Rice Gooch. Their great-grandson Dr. Allen Goodman Gooch served as an assistant surgeon in 1862 in the Civil War. (Courtesy of Betty Williams Alzamora.)

This house, listed in the National Register of Historic Places, was built by the Morton family on a large farm on Nolensville Road north of the historic village. The kitchen and dining room were separated by a breezeway from the main house. Flour and sugar were hidden in storage during the Civil War. John and Kate Brittain purchased the house in 1890 and raised their seven children here, surviving a 1900 tornado that blew off the second story. (Courtesy of the Heritage Foundation.)

Slaves were brought to Tennessee with migrating families and were purchased in front of the county courthouse. Generations later, Frank Morton and Mattie Ridley raised their 12 children on their family-owned farm near York Road, which grew sorghum and corn as its biggest crops. As in many families, children were needed to work the farm and could not always attend school. As adults, several of the Mortons' children worked at other local farms and dairies. Mattie Ridley died in 1943. Frank died in 1953 and is buried in the black cemetery south of historic Nolensville. (Both, courtesy of the Nolensville Historic School.)

John Wesley York (1840–1907), a blacksmith and farmer, was one of three children born to James York, another North Carolina pioneer who settled land on what is now York Road. James married Elizabeth Merritt in Williamson County in 1830, and died in 1841. John Wesley York (left) married Rachel Margaret Chrisman (1845–1919) in 1860 and had eight children. Their son James R. (1862–1901) married Emma Jane (1869–1960). During World War I, four of their sons tried to serve but the Army would only take two of them, Charlie (1890–1961) and Eunice "Mammy" (1889–1967). Twins Walter (1895–1976) and Marvin (1895–1918) stayed in Nolensville. Marvin died in a farm accident during the war. Below, another son of John Wesley York, Ollie Mac York (1883–1961), is pictured with his wife, Sarah Pearl Neal (1885–1961), and four of their nine children around 1915. From left to right are Frank (1906–1958), Rachel on Ollie's lap, Norman, and Herman (1908–1994). (Both, courtesy of the York family.)

Benajah Hill McFarlin Sr. (1857–1922), at left above, was the son of Charles McFarlin (1830–1861) and Kate "Sallie" Gambill. The man on the right is unidentified. The McFarlin family came to the Nolensville area in 1819 and became large landowners. Benajah McFarlin Sr. purchased the William Kidd homeplace at the corner of Kidd and Nolensville Roads between 1907 and 1909. Son Benajah (or Benjamin) Hill McFarlin Jr. (1891–1979) served in World War I and was married to widow Evie Eliza Chrisman Goodloe (1891–1993). McFarlin was known for owning Greenvale Dairy, bought by Purity, as well as his Jack Barns, his initial ownership of the telephone company, and farming. Benajah McFarlin Sr. married Mary Jane Turner (1860–1952), right, and they had eight children. Turner's mother was Nancy Ann Guthrie, her father's second wife, who was descended from one of the earliest Tennessee families. Benajah Sr., "Daddy Mac," was known to be tough but could always be softened by the devoted wife he called "Brunettie." (Both, courtesy of Jim McFarlin.)

Martha Irvin Burke, shown in a c. 1850 tintype, was married to Thomas Harvey "T.H." Burke (1831–1910), grandson of Anson Burke (c. 1763–1840). Anson Burke brought three of his sons and his daughter to Tennessee in 1819. Martha and T.H. had five sons, all born in the Nolensville area named Burke Hollow. The hills, called knobs, made good vantage points in defending against Native American attacks. (Courtesy of Nelda Burke Vest.)

H.H. "Hub" Burke (1875–1963) and Kate Waters Burke (1883–1969), are holding Dan H. (left) and Carl J. Burke. Hub lived in the Burke Hollow home where he was born and operated a large farm. One of five sons of Civil War veteran T.H. (1831–1910) and Martha Irvin Burke, Hub was an elected constable, deputy sheriff, magistrate (1914), poorhouse commissioner (1916), and county truant officer. (Courtesy of Nelda Burke Vest.)

Ida Heithcock Burke (1882–1984) is pictured above in 1912 holding Zelma. Standing from left to right are Lucy, Russell, Molly, and Catherine. Ida was married to James Ransom Burke (1880–1969); the family descended from Anson Burke and lived in Burke Hollow with their nine children. The clothes are sewn from fabric and not flour sack material, confirming that they are pictured prior to the Depression. At right, Ida is on her back porch around 1950. (Both, courtesy of Betty Jenkins Hughes and Frances Burke Stephens.)

Mary Elizabeth (Lizzie) Irvin Burke of Burke Hollow (1838–1919) is pictured with granddaughter Erma Agnes Jenkins (1904–1997) about 1911. Erma is pouting because she did not want to wear the bow in her hair. Mount Zion Church, located in Burke Hollow, was torn down in 1863 by Union soldiers to build the signal station on Daddy's Knob with a clear view of Murfreesboro and Franklin. Church members went to Trinity Church, which received compensation by the US government in 1907 for the loss. (Courtesy of Erma Jenkins Hunter.)

Sara Lenora Burke Jenkins (1874–1965) and her husband, Joe Jenkins (1868–1941), pose with family around 1896. Baby Emmett (1895–1985) is on Lenora's lap holding a pocketknife. Lenora's mother, Mary Elizabeth Irvin Burke, is seated at left, and standing from left to right are brothers John Franklin Burke, Charles Anson Burke holding Lenora's son Johnny (1894–1943), and Joe Jenkins. Lenora had seven children. Her father, Charles Anson Burke (1870–1912), passed away when she was 10 years old. (Courtesy of Lillian B. Jenkins and Betty Jenkins Hughes.)

Joseph Smith's (1846–1912) ancestors came to the Nolensville area in 1810. He married Lorella Coleman Smith (1853–1950), and the family joined Mount Olivet Methodist Episcopal Church South, for which Joseph would serve as a steward. He was a farmer, sheriff's deputy, and notary public. The Smith homestead was on Sunset Road. Daughter Cleo Smith (Battle) taught at Split Log School in the early 1900s. (Courtesy of Carolyn Hughes Battle.)

Nancy Louisa Tennessee Mildred Dolyon Elyon Colyon Pope married J.K. Pope in 1866 and was known as Louisa. Five generations of Pope women have lived on the property known as Hicklen Farm with the marriage of Sarah Woods (the fourth generation) to A.B. "Johnny" Hicklen. The farm, which ran a beloved pumpkin patch on Rocky Fork Road, includes logs from a two-room cabin on the property that was added to a barn. The original smokehouse, outhouse, and chicken coop still stand. The family is preserving the property in a land trust. (Courtesy of the Hicklens.)

Accomplished artist Minnie Alice Mauldin (Jenkins) (1880–1960), a great-great-granddaughter of a Revolutionary War soldier and raised in Water Valley, Mississippi, is pictured at age 17 on the far right with her fellow art students. Sadie Mauldin is third from the left, and Alice Backstrom is fourth from the right. (Courtesy of Donald Jenkins.)

Minnie Alice Mauldin, from an established family, is pictured in her wedding dress in 1905. Known as Alice, she married Elmer Sherwood Jenkins (1876–1969), an educator who had served as principal of Nolensville Academy before traveling with a group of Peabody colleagues to teach at Water Valley Military Academy in 1902. He later became school superintendent in Lake Charles, Louisiana. As a married couple, they returned to Nolensville in 1914 with their young son Jim, born in 1908. (Courtesy of Donald Jenkins.)

Alice engaged with agricultural life on the Jenkins dairy and cattle farm south of town on Nolensville Road while continuing to paint. Her husband, Elmer Sherwood Jenkins, an educator and great-great-grandson of settler Green Jenkins, made every task a lesson for their only son, James Sherwood Jenkins (1908–1991). An avid reader, Elmer was fluent in four languages and enjoyed discussions with clergy and others on his studies, which included study of the Bible. (Courtesy of Donald Jenkins.)

Participating in a Nolensville ladies' bridge club, Alice, with her genteel roots, entertained with her finest wares and gave one of her smaller paintings to the winner of the game. Paintings of all sizes remain in the family and have varied, but primarily floral, themes. Some date to 1897. (Courtesy of Donald Jenkins.)

Descendants of Henry Williams and Mary Gooch Williams who came to Nolensville in the 1800s, the William Cass Williams family had 800 acres on York Road. Pictured in 1915 are, from left to right, eight-year-old Marshall DeWitt on the horse, William Cass (1849–1932), Frank Yeargin, 14-year-old Bailey Key, 11-year-old William Gale, Mary Clara (or Clair) Yeargin Cass (1859–1940), and four-year-old Louis Cass. William and Clara were married in 1881. (Courtesy of Betty Williams Alzamora.)

Sherwood Green "S.G." Jenkins (1843–1915) is the grandson of Green Jenkins, who initially came to Nolensville in 1780 with a surveying crew. Green Jenkins returned to Warren County, North Carolina, and married Sally Green, kin to Nolensville settler Sherwood Green, in 1802. They had five children, including Marmaduke Jenkins, father of S.G. Jenkins, and returned to Nolensville by oxcart in the early 1800s. (Courtesy of Donald Jenkins.)

Two

WAR AND RESILIENCE

When the Civil War broke out in 1861, Williamson County was the third wealthiest in Tennessee. Sympathies were split, and the state was the last to secede from the Union. It was also the first to rejoin it after the war. Tobacco, cattle, and grain were popular crops in Middle Tennessee on land worked by farmers and slaves. By 1860, there were 275,719 slaves living in Tennessee, which was a quarter of the state's population. The average Nolensville farm had one to five slaves.

Nolensville was not a battle site, but like other areas, skirmishes occurred and the Union occupied Tennessee as early as 1862. Residents hid horses or food lest they be stolen, and churches were damaged or destroyed by both sides. One woman in Burke Hollow craftily took hair from her horse's tail to bind the leg up so it would appear lame. As a result, a Union soldier did not take her horse. Many men from the area served in the 20th and 24th Tennessee Regiments. Just as the state was divided, there were a few Union sympathizers in Nolensville. A local Confederate soldier was tortured to death, his vengeful cousin caught, and a Union wagon train and prisoners captured while residents fought to survive. Peace came, and farmers and former slaves rebuilt the agrarian economy and Nolensville's places of worship. In 1869, African Americans received land for their own church.

The town lost businesses and its farms scraped by during the Depression. The small village would send many of its sons to serve in foreign wars. After World War II, Nolensville became a place to rest and rebuild lives. A newcomer who survived incredible odds as a prisoner of war found life again here on a farm. Devastating fires of the 1950s and 1960s reshaped the historic district and prompted residents to action, eventually building a fire department in the 1970s. Resilience runs through every Nolensville farm, family, and business. Whether in war or peace, the small community figured out new ways to meet challenges. The following stories never stand alone but represent the lives of many Nolensville families.

Born in 1843, S.G. Jenkins (see page 24) was orphaned at 14 and sent to work for his uncle Wash Kidd. He joined the 4th Tennessee Cavalry at 18 and served four years. In order to join the cavalry, enlisted men had to supply their own horse and gun. Shown in his Confederate uniform, he was not pleased to have to hold Union guns for this photograph. His formal education had ended in fourth grade, but he went on to own many businesses in town and was president of the Bank of Nolensville from its start in 1906 to his death in 1915. He was buried in his Confederate uniform. (Courtesy of Donald Jenkins.)

Charlotte Jane Fowlkes Jenkins (1848–1924) was a descendant of a Revolutionary War soldier. She married S.G. Jenkins in 1870 and had nine children. (Courtesy of Donald Jenkins.)

Thomas Benton Smith, born in 1838, was from the Triune-Nolensville area and was an officer in the 20th Tennessee Infantry Regiment. He fought in battles at Stones River and Franklin and was beaten as a prisoner in 1864 at the Battle of Nashville. In 1886, he was admitted to an asylum for depression and mania, which may have stemmed from brain damage when he was a prisoner. He was treated there until his death in 1923. (Courtesy of TSLA.)

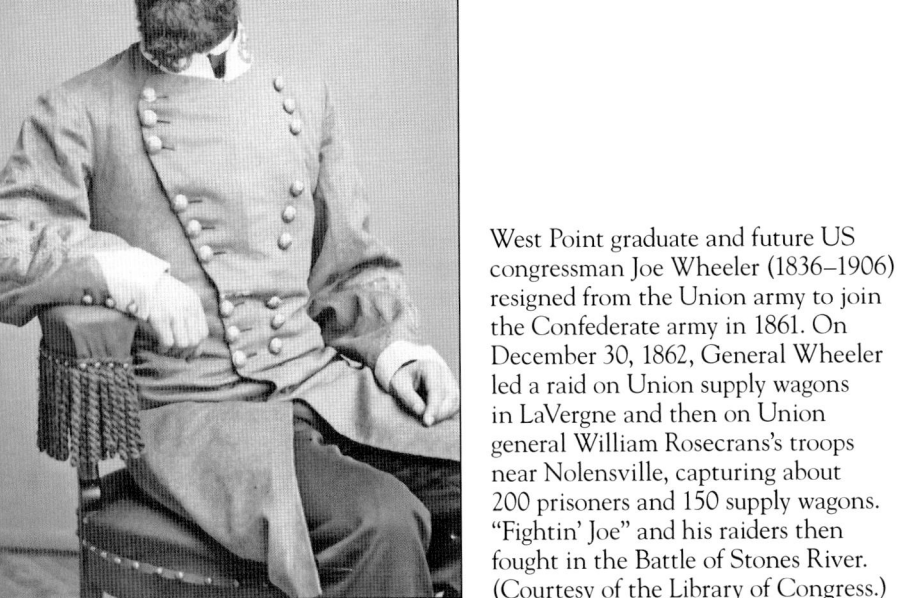

West Point graduate and future US congressman Joe Wheeler (1836–1906) resigned from the Union army to join the Confederate army in 1861. On December 30, 1862, General Wheeler led a raid on Union supply wagons in LaVergne and then on Union general William Rosecrans's troops near Nolensville, capturing about 200 prisoners and 150 supply wagons. "Fightin' Joe" and his raiders then fought in the Battle of Stones River. (Courtesy of the Library of Congress.)

Dewitt Smith Jobe (1840–1864), pictured, and Dewitt Smith (1843–1864) were cousins of Thomas Benton Smith. Jobe enlisted in 1861 into the Zollicoffer Guards, which became the 20th Tennessee Regiment, Company B, and included Nolensvillians. Jobe became a Coleman Scout, working behind Union lines. In 1864, he was caught in a Nolensville field, so he swallowed the secret information. Union soldiers put out his eyes, cut off his tongue, and dragged him to death behind a horse. One of the Jobe family's slaves, Frank Jobe, retrieved his body for burial off of Rocky Fork Road. (Courtesy of TSLA.)

When Dewitt Smith heard of the torture and death of his cousin, he left his regiment near Chattanooga to get revenge. He slit the throats of 14 Union soldiers as they slept and killed about 50 within two months. Captured near Nolensville, he died from injuries. (Courtesy of TSLA.)

Sherwood Green's youngest son, Edward Green (1830–1901), a Confederate soldier married to Mary Louise King (1837–1922), fought alongside Georgia native William Carlton "Brick" Smith (1847–1912). The two were nearly captured in Union-occupied Nolensville at the Sherwood Green home, where they came for provisions. Mary Louise reportedly refused to open the door for the home to be searched. Before the door could be broken down, she opened it and aimed her weapon at the Union soldiers, and they left. Edward's brother Sherwood Green Jr. and neighbor John W. King both died as soldiers in Atlanta on August 24, 1864. Smith returned to Nolensville years later and in 1886 married Ed and Louise's daughter Mary Sue Green (1859–1926). Nolensvillians served in the 20th and 24th Tennessee Regiments. Shown below, the 24th Tennessee Regiment, Company B, reunites after the war. (Above, courtesy of Janice Page Green; below, courtesy of Nelda Burke Vest.)

Fannie Battle (1842–1924) was a daughter of Confederate colonel Joel A. Battle, who organized soldiers from the Nolensville area into what would become the 20th Tennessee Regiment. The Battle family lived in the Cane Ridge and Nolensville area. Fannie, who rarely spoke of her war experience, was a Confederate scout who would cross Union lines to get information. Arrested in 1863 at the age of 20 as a spy, she went to prison in the North. Her fiancé and two brothers were killed, another brother and her father were captured, and the family home was burned. Through negotiation, she was exchanged for four Union soldiers. After the war, she taught in Nashville schools for 16 years and volunteered with the Nashville Relief Society. In 1886, her only choice after a night of prayer was to "give up school teaching and throw my life, all of it, into the work." Before she died in 1924, she had fundraised, pushed reforms, and organized to open the state's first day care, a nursing home, and a myriad of social services. The Fannie Battle Day Home was named in 1921. (Courtesy of Nashville Public Library.)

A US Army tank parks on Kidd/Battle Road during maneuvers in 1943. From 1941 to 1944, some 850,000 soldiers practiced military maneuvers in Middle Tennessee. Tanks traveled Nolensville Road, turning on Kidd Road to get to the woods between Kidd and Rocky Fork Roads. Residents, limited by war rations, would still bring the soldiers food and coffee. Lucky kids got to climb on the tanks and get a chocolate from a soldier. (Courtesy of Carolyn Hughes Battle.)

J.T. Williams (1919–2001), an engineer and top turret gunner, shown here about 1945 inside a B-17, made 35 bombing attacks on Nazi military and industrial targets. He married Mary Sherwood Brittain (1917–1989) in 1936. Back home in Nolensville, he did not talk about World War II much and was a successful businessman. He did buy a little Piper Cub to fly and would sometimes buzz Nolensville. (Courtesy of Peggy Williams Taylor and Kaye Williams Burns.)

Wilburn Jenkins (1922–1967), far right, is pictured home on leave in 1942 with his family. From left to right are brother Edward (1924–2014), parents Ruth (1905–1998) and Emmett Jenkins (1895–1985), and sisters Betty (with garrison cap) and Agnes, in Burke Hollow. Jenkins was related to the Burke men, seven from the same family, who also served during World War II. All returned except for Robert Shannon Burke (1925–1944), who was killed in France in 1944. Robert Shannon's third cousin, Vance Givens Burke (1925–1942), was serving as a flight instructor in Jackson, Tennessee, when he died. (Courtesy of Betty J. Hughes.)

Melvin "Cap" and Audrey Sanders reunite after World War II. Audrey made her sailor dress for the occasion. The couple rented and then purchased the home at the corner of Nolensville and Clovercroft Roads. After she was widowed, Audrey lived there until she passed away at 90. That home later became Nolensville Toy Shop. This photograph inspired the creation of Nolensville's Veterans Day Parade. (Courtesy of Beth Lothers.)

Sam Donald Road is named after Maj. Sam Donald, one of the longest-held prisoners of war in World War II. Donald, of Virginia, was a minister and became an Army chaplain in 1939. While he was serving in Bataan, Philippines, the province surrendered to Japan in the spring of 1942. Donald survived the 125-mile Bataan Death March, and during his first two months as a prisoner, conducted services for 2,700 Americans who died by starvation or by bayonet. Prisoners who survived a horrendous cargo ship transfer to an island in 1944 worked in harsh conditions with poor food. Men who died there were cremated, and Donald conducted the services. With the end of the war, Sam Donald finally gained his freedom. The telegram below was sent to his mother, Ida, informing her he was alive and no longer a prisoner of war. (Both, courtesy of the Robin and Sara Miller family.)

CLASS OF SERVICE

This is a full-rate Telegram or Cablegram unless its deferred character is indicated by a suitable symbol above or preceding the address.

WESTERN UNION

A. N. WILLIAMS
PRESIDENT

1201

SYMBOLS

DL=Day Letter
NL=Night Letter
LC=Deferred Cable
NLT=Cable Night Letter
Ship Radiogram

The filing time shown in the date line on telegrams and day letters is STANDARD TIME at point of origin. Time of receipt is STANDARD TIME at point of destination

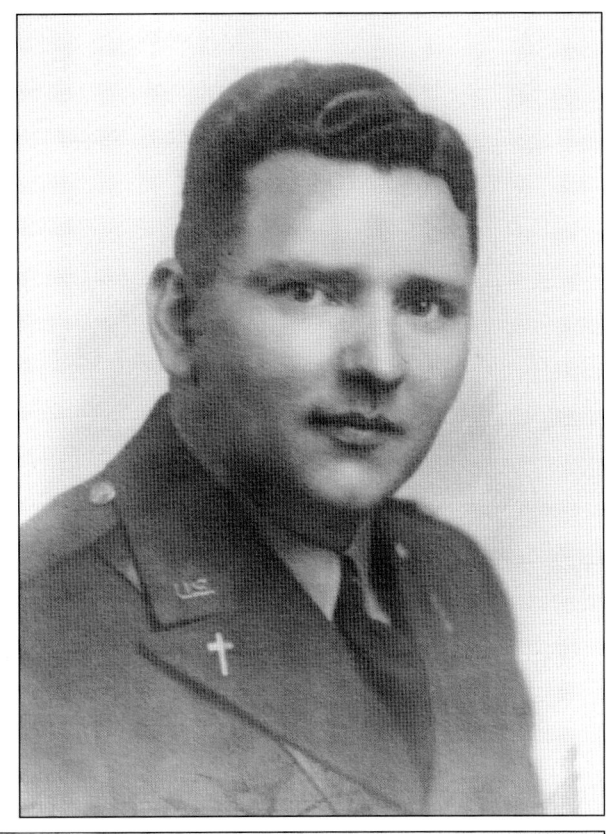

RU23 46 GOVT=WUX WASHINGTON DC SEP 4 304PM

MRS IDA M DONALD=
701 PINE ST FN=

THE SECRETARY OF WAR HAS ASKED ME TO INFORM YOU THAT YOUR SON CAPTAIN SAMUEL E DONALD ZERO TWO TWO SEVEN FIVE ZERO IS ALIVE AND WELL AS OF TWENTY FIVE APRIL NINETEEN FORTY FIVE AND IS NO LONGER A PRISONER OF WAR AS PREVIOUSLY REPORTED=
=EDWARD F WITSELL ACTING THE ADJUTANT GENERAL OF THE ARMY.

9OOAM SEP 5

THE COMPANY WILL APPRECIATE SUGGESTIONS FROM ITS PATRONS CONCERNING ITS SERVICE

After the war, Sam Donald spent six months in a Virginia hospital and married Vi Taylor, whom he met before the war. The couple traveled, ending up in Nolensville, where they bought a farm in 1949 on what would later be named Sam Donald Road. Donald had a lake built, which was credited with helping save his cattle in the summer drought of 1952. They sold in 1986, and unfortunately, this house burned in 2018. (Courtesy of the Robin and Sara Miller family.)

Donald, shown in 1959, later wrote, "My wife and I worked hard and built the farm and raised cattle and enjoyed living the 'life of Riley' among the good people of Nolensville." At Nolensville First United Methodist Church, he taught and organized a men's class with Roy Hughes and Teddy Williams. In 1987, Donald was honored at a presentation surrounded by a dozen Nolensville veterans. He died in 1995 at age 85. (Courtesy of the Robin and Sara Miller family.)

Fire ravaged the historic district for the third time in 1968, leveling J.B. Ozburn's grain storage and another of his buildings, the Williams grocery, and for the second time, Ed House's barbershop and small apartment. This *Nashville Banner* photograph was taken from behind the destruction on the west side of Nolensville Road, looking out at the road. A 1953 fire had destroyed the Waller funeral home, a garage and egg candling building, and Ed House's barbershop and home on the west side. The funeral home would rebuild. A 1954 fire destroyed A.C. Brown's restaurant, home, and bus stop on the east side of the street. At right, the two-story brick former "bank building" was spared. The advertisement for "Williams Lunch" at the top of the building can also be seen above on the left in the aftermath of the 1968 fire. (Above, courtesy of Nashville Banner Collection at Nashville Library; right, courtesy of Carrie Stephenson Ozburn and Peggy Stephenson Wilson.)

With each fire, firefighters from Nashville and Franklin pumped water from Mill Creek, which helped save the town from even worse destruction. In 1974, the Nolensville Jaycees worked to establish a volunteer fire department. Dallas Johnson (front) mixes concrete with Pete Mosley to build a fire station behind what was then Bill Johnson's Gulf station on Nolensville Road. Johnson donated the land for the fire station and serviced the fire trucks. In its first year, the department answered 19 calls. Pete Mosley was the first fire chief, and Presley Hughes followed, serving for 37 years. The work to establish the department was awarded nationally by the Jaycees. Williamson County built a new station house for the volunteer department in 1991. These garages became part of Nolensville Auto Care. (Both, courtesy of Presley Hughes.)

Three

HEART OF A TOWN

Since the 1800s, free enterprise has reigned on less than a mile stretch of Nolensville Road. The small business district at the heart of the village has Mill Creek gently flowing behind its east side. A bank, several grocery stores, liveries, wheel and feed stores, hotels, churches, a carriage shop and funeral home, and more filled the street. The first doctor's office in Nolensville operated in the cottage behind A Home Place Bed-and-Breakfast, formerly the Stagecoach Inn. Some of Nolensville's historic structures still stand and have been repurposed by new entrepreneurs. In the beginning, town buildings were tight together, often almost on top of each other. Fires in 1953, 1954, and 1968 changed the streetscape. While some businesses, such as the Waller Funeral Home and Williams grocery, rebuilt, others did not. The gaps left between became necessary parking lots.

At the turn of the 20th century, the invention of the telephone changed the way of life in Nolensville. The first telephone switchboard was located at the home of the Ozburns in the middle of town, which has since become retail space. In the 1930s, B.H. McFarlin assumed ownership of the telephone company, and then Allen Green bought the stock. Green moved the switchboard to his home on the corner of Old Clovercroft and Nolensville Roads. The Cities Telephone Company relocated to a brick building nearby. In 1960, United Telephone purchased the company. Amelia Ozment Hayes recalls working the switchboard overnight as a teenager with her protective father sleeping on the floor.

Rural electricity cooperatives owned by members turned the lights on in Nolensville beginning in the 1920s. Gas also came to Nolensville about the same time. The Nolensville–College Grove Utility District, with its first office located in a trailer in the 1960s, worked to make water available to homes and businesses so artesian wells no longer had to be drawn from and directed to nearby buildings. Accessible sewer services to the Nolensville area would not come until large sewer lines connected to Nashville along Nolensville Road in the 1990s.

Built on the banks of Mill Creek, Nolensville business was robust in the early 1900s. The book *Goodspeed History of Tennessee 1886* noted that "Nolensville has a large number of businesses for a place of its size." Looking north on the dirt road, on the left are the J.A. Williams & Co./ Osborne store, a livery, and a wheel store. The brick building, which still stands, was the Bank of Nolensville. (Courtesy of the Jessie Burke Sealy family.)

Nolensville Road is shown in the early 1900s at the south end of town looking north. Buildings on the right side included a drugstore and a blacksmith shop where the buggy is parked. Decades later, that area became home to Johnson's Gulf station, which later became Nolensville Auto Care. Also seen is Putman's store, a building that has been repurposed as various stores and shops. (Courtesy of Carrie Stephenson Ozburn and Peggy Stephenson Wilson.)

Rayden Smith (left) and Ted Jenkins talk behind the post office that sat on the east side of the road about 1920. The person gesturing on the right is unidentified. Years earlier, in 1868, S.G. Jenkins bought this building for $40 and ran a saloon here. Nolensville's first post office was established about 1820–1822. The post office had several locations in the historic district. (Courtesy of Larry Williams.)

Ted Jenkins sits on the porch of the post office about 1920. By 1861, a horse-drawn mail route, detailed in the *Nashville Union and American*, went from Nashville to Shelbyville, passing through Nolensville and Triune. It departed Nashville at 7:00 a.m. on Tuesday, Thursday, and Saturday. Fire destroyed many of the old postal locations. The post office was moved to Oldham Road in 1962 with Frank Wilson as postmaster, who decades later was named national Postmaster of the Year. (Courtesy of Larry Williams.)

ASK YOUR GROCER FOR
Williamson County
BUTTER

It Is Manufactured and Marketed By The
Nolensville Co-operative Creamery
Nolensville, Tennessee
"Williamson County" Butter took first prize at the 1931 Tenn. State Fair
Nearly 500,000 pounds marketed during year 1935.
It Is Made Right
And Made Right Here at Home
Nolensville Co-operative Creamery
Nolensville, Tennessee

Nolensville Co-Operative Creamery quickly established itself after opening in 1921. By 1923, it had packed and shipped approximately 200,000 pounds of butter throughout the South, paying a six-percent dividend to its stockholders, according to a *Review Appeal* story headlined "Progressive Creamery at Nolensville a Big Asset." The ad shown hear states that nearly 500,000 pounds of butter were marketed during 1935. (Courtesy of the Nolensville Historic School.)

The Nolensville Co-Operative Creamery, owned and controlled by the farmers, had as its slogan "better cream made into better butter," according to a 1951 story in *The Nashville Tennessean*. By that year, Ben R. Gant had managed the creamery for 28 years. Three trucks picked up cream from farms in Williamson and surrounding counties. The creamery operated until 1957. The building has been repurposed as antique and gift stores. (Courtesy of the Williamson County Archives.)

Creamery workers stand behind a 600-pound block of butter. At left is plant manager John Vernon. Behind him is manager Ben Gant. Vernon would give cream a taste and nose test to detect any unusual feed or water. After pasteurization, it churned in the drum for 30 minutes, and buttermilk drained. After water rinses, salting, and moisture tests, the block was chilled and then cut into quarter pounds. (Courtesy of the Vernon family.)

Mill Creek influenced William Nolen to stay and later stake his claim on the 120 acres that includes the town bearing his name. Nolensville Road follows the creek, which has overtaken its banks on several occasions. Major floods swept through town in 1979, 1984, and 2010. If not for pumping the creek's water, fires in 1953, 1954, and 1968 would have destroyed more of the town than they did. (Courtesy of Kent Travis.)

This mill was built on Nolensville Road about 1932–1933 by Owen Allen Gooch. The original four-story mill was built by John A. Jordan before the Civil War in Arrington and was initially intended to be used as a whiskey distillery. After changing ownership many times, a group of stockholders moved the Arrington mill to another Nolensville location by wagon in 1890. After it burned in 1931, Gooch built this mill in the historic village. Originally a flour mill, the business evolved into a feed mill as the demand for flour waned, especially after this smaller mill was built. Below, Pete Vernon (left) and David Gooch (the owner since 1959) take a minute to relax at the Nolensville Milling Company in the 1970s. The mill sold feed and other supplies for farmers until it closed in 2006. The historic building was repurposed as an Amish market and deli. (Above, illustration by John Strasser; below, courtesy of Joe Horton Studio's Nashville Historic Prints Collection.)

Looking south in 1901, the man on the left is identified as John "Jack" Burke next to the King Hotel, the two-story building on the left. Burke (1877–1939) ran the hotel and the livery stable across the street for a time. The man on the far right on the porch of a store is identified as S.G. Jenkins, who was president of the bank that occupied the two-story brick building on the right. (Courtesy of Jessie Burke Sealy family.)

The Benjamin Tarver King family stands on the porch of the hotel that fronted Nolensville Road. From left to right are unidentified, Benjamin Tarver King and his wife, Susan, and daughter Mary Louise King Green. The hotel was known as King's Inn, King's Tavern, and later Nolensville Hotel. In disrepair, this hotel was torn down in 1968. (Courtesy of the Heritage Foundation.)

Nolensville Hotel, formerly known as King's Inn, was a resting place for stagecoaches, wagon masters, drummers, and other travelers. Horses were changed and stabled in the livery across Nolensville Road. Here, a shadow crosses Nolensville Road, making it falsely appear as if a long driveway leads to the hotel. The hotel was actually very close to Nolensville Road. Below, Billy Osburn "B.O." (left) and Horace S. Williams, shown about 1925, operated a general store and gas station next to the hotel, seen on the left. In 1954, when this building was a restaurant run by A.C. "Farmer" Brown, it burned. (Above, courtesy of Peggy Stephenson Wilson and Carrie Stephenson Ozburn; below, illustration by John Strasser.)

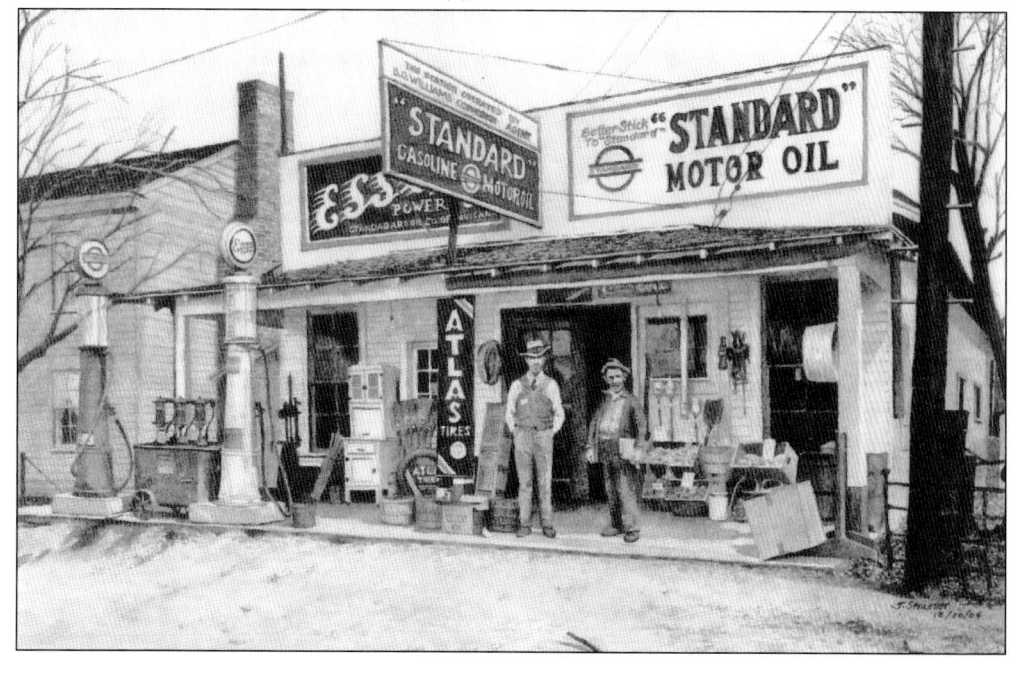

Howard and Sally Putman lived in this home next to their store. This building had also been known as the Stagecoach Inn. About 60 years later, the home was in disrepair. Alfred and Evelyn Bennett bought the house at auction in 1989 while visiting Nolensville on a weekend. The floor and ceiling were falling in, but the Bennetts restored its beauty, creating a home and a bed-and-breakfast. (Courtesy of Rev. Alfred and Evelyn Bennett.)

In 1923, owner Howard Putman stands with family and others in his dry goods store. From left to right are Putman, Henry Haley, W.A. "Buck" Hall, Will Putman, and J.J. Putman. The boys in front are William Vance Putman and Johnny Hodge. Ed Thomas ran a grocery store here for three decades into the 1980s. This building would later be repurposed as various types of shops. (Courtesy of Debbie Suttmiller.)

Johnson's Gulf station is shown above in the 1950s. Bill Johnson, who owned the auto garage across the street, bought this lot in the early 1950s. After building it up to be on higher ground, he opened a Gulf gas station in 1952. In the historic district, this is the only building that has been continuously used for the same type of business. Melvin "Cap" Sanders ran it until 1985. Donnie Bryan started doing business here in 1996 as Nolensville Auto Care and bought the property in the early 2000s. Below, Nolensville businesses are shown in 1912. Businesses on the right side (the east side of Nolensville Road) back up to Mill Creek. A portion of the businesses on the left side (the west side of Nolensville Road) back up to a tributary and flood plain. (Above, courtesy of Sandra Johnson; below, courtesy of TSLA.)

Situated on Nolen's 1818 lot No. 7, this home stood beside Nolensville First United Methodist Church. It is believed to have been used as a Civil War hospital. Sold by Dr. Tom McMurray in 1884 for a parsonage, purchased by J.J. Jackson in 1905, and sold to Clyde Tucker in the 1940s, the home's blood-stained wood floor with bullet holes remained until it was torn down in 1982. (Courtesy of Scott York.)

In 1901, Mount Olivet Methodist Episcopal Church South placed a bell in its 75-foot steeple. Shown in 1940, the church had changed its name the previous year to Nolensville Methodist Church, and it eventually became Nolensville First United Methodist Church. A fundraiser in the 2000s restored the landmark red steeple. A basement was added in the 1930s, classrooms in the 1950s and 1970s, and a fellowship hall in 2000. (Courtesy of Carrie Stephenson Ozburn.)

Pictured at the Old Carmichael Place next to the Nolensville cemetery in the early 1900s are, from left to right, unidentified, Mamie Carmichael (1871–1936), and Martha Priscilla Jenkins Carmichael (1848–1939). A front porch was added later. The home, most likely built between 1880 and 1890, has been used for a veterinary specialist's office and a salon. (Courtesy of Carrie Stephenson Ozburn and Peggy Stephenson Wilson.)

The James and Lillie Carmichael Williams home is situated beside the Old Carmichael Place. Pictured in 1905 are Pearl Tennyson on the steps, Mamie (left) and Addie Carmichael standing, and Mattie Carmichael holding Herman Williams beside Lillie C. Williams. Martha Williams and dog Shepp are sitting on the grass. The King family owned this home at one time. The private home has been renovated over the years. (Courtesy of Carrie Stephenson Ozburn.)

Emmitt (1878–1938) and Dolly Fly Williams and children were the first residents of this home on the corner of Old Clovercroft Road and Nolensville Road. J.W. Williams had earlier built another house for Emmitt and Dolly, but she did not like it, so he built this home in the early 1900s. Above, the home is shown on February 11, 1910, when 12 inches of snow fell. A lot of the land in front would be taken by the paving of Nolensville Road in 1929–1931. Below, Dolly Williams and her daughter Louise display an American flag in the front yard. Allen Johnson Green (1894–1968) owned the home during the time the telephone switchboard was moved here. Cap and Audrey Sanders last owned the home until it was renovated in the 2000s into a law office and toy shop. (Above, courtesy of Heather Bell; below, courtesy of Marjorie Ragsdale Hernandez.)

J.B. Ozburn, a Nolensville business owner, owned this house during the mid-1900s. The property was first sold in 1871. Also known as the Bateman place, it housed the first telephone operator station in Nolensville. The switchboard operation was in three different locations over the years, including the house across Old Clovercroft Road and in a small building behind it. This building has been repurposed as antique and gift shops. (Courtesy of Carrie Stephenson Ozburn.)

Thomason Motor Company opened in 1919. J.S. Thomason lived in the home just visible between the garage and the Williams home at left. J.A. Williams was a business partner. His children, Annis Williams (middle) and Herman Williams (right) stand outside with Sissie Ellis. A Chevrolet dealership, it closed during World War II. In 1946, Bill Johnson opened his garage here. The building has been repurposed as retail and antique stores. (Courtesy of Carrie Stephenson Ozburn.)

In the 1950s, Bill Johnson started building race cars, and he owned at least three cars that saw much success, including No. 23, shown here with Johnson (left) and driver Pete Eudailey. Drivers Frank Reed and Jimmy Griggs raced his other cars. He built stock cars for other owners through the early 1960s to race on short dirt tracks in Tennessee, Alabama, and Kentucky. In the late 1950s, several of his cars raced the sand track at Daytona Beach. Below, Johnson, after his discharge from the military in 1945, bought this garage with his father George Dallas Johnson. In 1974, Johnson let the new volunteer fire department use it to store its first fire truck, which he also serviced for free. Parked outside during the day, he moved it inside at night, giving keys to a few firefighters in case of a night call. This building has also been repurposed as retail and antique stores. (Above, courtesy of Sandra Johnson; below, courtesy of Presley Hughes.)

B.O. and Horace S. Williams owned a general store. B.O. Williams is on the left, leaning against the telephone in this 1920s photograph. (Courtesy of Kaye Williams Burns and Peggy Williams Taylor.)

In August 1954, Will Sanders (left) joins Horace Williams on the bench at the Williams store on the west side of Nolensville Road. The store was often a gathering place to catch up on community news. Horace's granddaughters Kaye and Peggy remember as girls roller skating on this porch and doing homework in the back next to a coal stove. (Courtesy of Kaye Williams Burns and Peggy Williams Taylor.)

At right, Ed House cuts Jim Ozburn's hair in 1959. Known as Peggy because he had one leg, House gave 50¢ haircuts, with the same style for all. He always gave a dime back to kids so they could buy a cold drink. His first barbershop burned in the fire of 1953, and this shop, his second, burned in 1968 along with the Williams store and several other buildings. The store was rebuilt by the Williams family. Below, from left to right, James Ridley, Nuel Jordan, George Morton, and Jonas Morton gather outside the Williams store in the 1970s or 1980s. In recent decades, this building has been a grocery store and restaurants. (Right, courtesy of Carrie Stephenson Ozburn; below, courtesy of the Nolensville Historic School.)

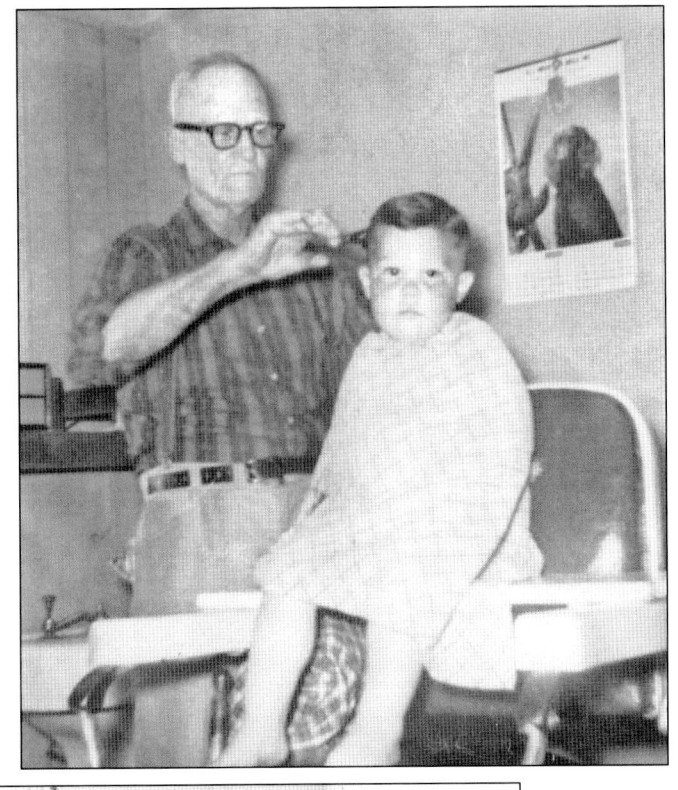

The J.W. Williams & Son store, known as the Wheel Store, is shown in these early 1900s photographs. Williams (1848–1940), a large landowner, was a partner in several stores with his sons. In 1881, Williams bought the King Hotel (shown on page 43) and livery, owning them for several years. He was also one of the founders of the Bank of Nolensville in 1906. Maud Williams ran a pool hall, bowling alley, and dance hall here in the 1930s. (Both, courtesy of Larry Williams.)

J.B. Ozburn operated a general merchandise and feed store on the west side of the business district. In the early 1900s, it had been the J.A. Williams store (see page 38). At one time, it had dirt floors and was used as a voting location. It was also the location of the Puckett-Thomas Grocery in 1947. Ed Thomas would go on to run his own store across the street in what had been the Putman store. An office on the left was once the post office. This building burned in 1968, and the area became a parking lot for other businesses. Below, Horace Williams cranks the old Williams truck he is using to haul hay in front of what was the original livery stable. (Above, courtesy of Carrie Stephenson Ozburn; below, courtesy of Peggy Williams Taylor and Kaye Williams Burns.)

The Bank of Nolensville was opened in 1906 by S.G. Jenkins, who was president until his death in 1915. It was then managed by Williams family members and is shown here about 1920 with president Walter Parks Kimery. Listed in the National Register of Historic Places, the bank survived an attempted robbery in the 1920s, but like many others, it failed in 1932 during the Depression. Later, this building became home to businesses and shops. (Courtesy of Larry Williams.)

Nolensville businessmen and their sons pose in 1897. From left to right are (first row) Dr. B.E. Green, Ben Waller, Emmitt Williams, Jim Williams, Dr. D.R. Gooch, Jim Carmichael, Charlie Waller, child Charles Edward Smith, W.C. "Brick" Smith, and A.J. Green: (second row) Eugene Vincent, Fed Jenkins, Tom Green, Jim Neise, John Smith, Will Williams, Joe Jenkins, Will Davis, Bob Gooch, and S.G. Jenkins. (Courtesy of Donald Jenkins.)

B.O. Williams Sr. (1893–1968), a veteran of World War I and son of J.W. Williams and Louise Hume Osburn, operated general merchandise stores in Nolensville for decades. He had one son, Billy Osburn Jr. (1920–1980), with his first wife, Alma Butts (1895–1949). Below, he ran this B.O. Williams store adjacent to the bank building with his wife, known fondly as "Miss Alma." B.O. Williams Sr. died after a fall on the ice at his home. After his death, son Billy O. Williams Jr. and other family members ran the store. (Right, courtesy of Larry Williams; below, courtesy of Carrie Stephenson Ozburn and Peggy Stephenson Wilson.)

A Falstaff Beer sign hangs above the doorway at the B.O. Williams store, where soft drinks and beer were served. Several beer joints were positioned along Nolensville Road, which for decades had a not-so-savory reputation. National Prohibition was repealed in the early 1930s, but Williamson County waited until 1939 to allow the sale of liquor and restricted it to downtown Franklin. Bootlegging happened around the county, especially in rural areas. Blacks and whites were separate to an extent. Often, blacks would have to use the back or side doors at white-owned businesses. A black-owned beer joint was on Sunset Road. Below, the Waller Funeral Home, located north of the B.O. Williams store, used its Cadillac hearse as an ambulance to transport people to the hospital prior to the fire of 1953. (Above, courtesy of Larry Williams; below, courtesy of the Waller family.)

Since the 1800s, the Wallers made wagons, repaired buggies, housed blacksmith and cabinet shops, and sometimes made caskets. One of the oldest family-owned businesses in the county, the Wallers constantly evolved from carriage building to eventually directing a funeral home starting about 1873. The clapboard-covered, 100-plus-year-old funeral home was destroyed by fire in 1953, along with three other buildings on the west side of Nolensville Road. The Wallers rebuilt. After Mary Frances Waller Parrish's death in 2006, Woodbine Funeral Home owners bought it in 2007, restoring it as Waller Chapel. Below, the W.R. Waller & Son building is shown with a horse-drawn hearse used in the late 1800s. Ben E. Waller Sr. is driving. (Above, courtesy of Peggy Stephenson Wilson; below, courtesy of the Heritage Foundation.)

TOWN LOTS
AT
PUBLIC SALE!
NOLENSVILLE, TENN.
Saturday, August 15, 1914
SALE BEGINS PROMPTLY AT ONE O'CLOCK

Regardless of Price, We will Sell to the Highest Bidder about 30 of the

Most Beautiful Building Lots Ever to be Had in Nolensville

These lots are located in the Southwest part of town and known as the S. Jenkins land. You will never have another opportunity to buy choice building lots like these at your own price. Here is a chance to get a bargain for a home or for an investment.

TO THE BUSINESS MEN OF NOLENSVILLE: Come out and help us boost the good town of Nolensville. Don't be a knocker, but a booster. We come to boost your town, not to graft you. So come along and help us, which we are sure you will do.

$25.00 IN GOLD GIVEN AWAY FREE
BE SURE AND BE ON HAND

NOLENSVILLE is fifteen miles from Nashville, on the proposed extension of the Fourth Avenue car line, in one of the very best agricultural sections of the State. Its stable commercial business, splendid schools and churches, well-kept homes, good water, and the very best people, make Nolensville a very desirable place in which to live. It is second to none. Farmers, now is your time to buy a lot, move to town and educate your children. Buy while you can buy at your own price. There is a prosperous future for Nolensville, and lots are scarce and high. What better investment can you make than to buy one of these lots?

Is Real Estate Safe? Does Real Estate Pay? Stocks and bonds may decline and factories may burn, but REAL ESTATE IS ALWAYS THERE. Do you know that 95 per cent of real estate investments pay?—that 50 per cent of them double the money? What better investment can you make than to buy one of these building lots at your own price? Think it over carefully and act accordingly. Taking it all in all, you can't beat Nolensville. So come and buy one of these lots without fail.

DON'T FORGET THE DATE, SATURDAY, AUG. 15, 1914
The Ladies Are Especially Invited.   MUSIC BY THE BAND.

TERMS OF SALE: One-third cash, one-third six months, one-third twelve months. Six per cent interest from date on deferred payments, with bankable notes, or 2 per cent off for cash on deferred payments. For further information inquire at Nolensville Hotel.

OLIVER & WILKINSON
IGLEHART & REPPERT, Auctioners.

It's a Treat to Hear Them.   Bring Your Friends.

An advertisement for an auction of the "Most Beautiful Building Lots Ever to Be Had in Nolensville" details the big event happening on August 15, 1914, for land owned by S.G. Jenkins. Some of the small print reads: "Its stable commercial business, splendid schools and churches, well-kept homes, good water and the very best people make Nolensville a very desirable place in which to live. . . . There is a prosperous future for Nolensville and lots are scarce and high." With $25 in gold given away, ladies especially invited, and music by a band, it must have been quite an event. (Courtesy of Donald Jenkins.)

60

Four

ROAD TO EVERYWHERE

What was first a Native American trail became a dusty wagon and stagecoach route in the 1800s. The horse-ridden dirt road became a thoroughfare to Nashville with crude tollgate poles manually lifted after fees were paid. Automobiles paid tolls until the gates were removed in the mid-1920s. Long before Interstate 65 opened in 1958 and Interstate 24 was finished in 1968, travelers from north and south found a rest stop in Nolensville, with places to eat, sleep, or buy goods. A spoke of a wheel with Nashville as the center, Nolensville Road was a main corridor for travel.

Nolensville Road was once referred to as Fishing Ford because it crossed a ford at the low part of the Duck River near a fishing site. The trail stretched from Kentucky's Ohio River to Huntsville, Alabama, through Nolensville, becoming Nashville's Fourth Avenue in between. Once used by the Native Americans for commerce, war, and access to hunting grounds, it became a route used to attack settlers.

A 1787 account has troops from Nashville pursuing Native Americans who had killed three white settlers over Mill Creek on Fishing Ford. In 1813, Andrew Jackson traveled the road to fight the Creek Indians in Alabama.

Williamson County, formed in 1799, began clearing the trail and rocking the mud holes as early as 1807. Wagons and mules hauled rocks from a quarry to build the road in the 1830s–1840s. By 1856, the Nolensville Turnpike Company owned 26 miles of the roadway. Tollgate keepers collected fees about every five miles, with fees adjusted for funerals and ministers. A stagecoach could pay as much as $175 per year, with reductions for carrying US mail. Lawsuits were filed over injuries blamed on wagon wheels hitting rough surfaces.

By 1917, the Williamson County Commission began discussing buying out the controversial turnpikes. The Nolensville Turnpike Company refused the purchase price, and condemnation proceedings were issued in 1926. It was designated a state road and paved as State Route 11 in 1927; the route is also known as US 31A, Nashville Highway, Nolensville Pike, Nolensville Road, and Horton Highway farther south.

The humble beginnings of Nolensville Road are shown here in 1915, situated on Mill Creek's headwaters. Settlers along the creek grew a town with businesses near its banks including gristmills, sawmills, and molasses mills, along with a hotel, livery, and church. (Courtesy of Larry Williams.)

King's Inn, built in the early 1800s, was once operated by the Burke family. From left to right are unidentified, Raymond Burke, Bell Haley Burke and husband John Burke holding Jessie, and Mary Elizabeth Burke; in front are Houston (left) and Jack Burke. John (1877–1939) and Bell (1882–1977) ran this hotel and the livery stable across the street. The earliest innkeepers were Benjamin Tarver (1812–1889) and Susan Matthews King (1817–1875). (Courtesy of the Burke family.)

A.S. Ogilvie's stagecoach (above) made one daily trip from Chapel Hill to Nashville in 1894. The route was Nolensville Road, and Nolensville's business district was a perfect stop along the way with a hotel and livery for changing horses. The dusty roadway was once named Fishing Ford Road but became known as Nolensville Turnpike in the 1800s. The well-traveled dirt road became a toll road, hence the designation "pike," with tollgates every five miles. This turnpike system would continue into the late 1920s. Ogilvie (below) had stagecoaches to Nashville and Ashland City. Pictured is a stagecoach to Nolensville while at Rigg's Crossing in Chapel Hill. Passenger and mail service by stagecoach was common in the 19th century, and the coaches operated as late as 1910. (Above, courtesy of the Heritage Foundation; below, courtesy of Horton Studios.)

A system of railroads and turnpikes began in the 1800s. H.H. Burke (1875–1963), a foreman on the railroad, is seen on the far left above as part of the crew building a railroad overpass on Wilson Pike in 1912. Workers initially lived in a tent city. The College Grove depot, located 13 miles south of Nolensville, opened in 1914. The Lewisburg & Northern Railroad ran parallel to the highway, then northwest through Brentwood to Nashville. Early Nolensville property deeds reveal the railway's interest in connecting to Nolensville at one time. Below, tollgates on what became known as the Nolensville Turnpike were placed about every five miles. By 1924, the Williamson County government began purchasing toll roads in the county. Most owners negotiated; Wilson Pike was bought for $5,000 and Del Rio Pike for $4,250. (Above, courtesy of Nelda Burke Vest; below, courtesy of the Heritage Foundation.)

One of Nolensville's tollgates, possibly this one (above), was located at what longtime Nolensville locals call "Tollgate Hill." Nothing marks the area, as the old tollhouse burned down in the 1970s. The old tollgate stood on a hill two miles south of town, on the right side, across from 7512 Nolensville Road. While most owners sold, Tom Johnson (right), a bank president, appealed up to the Tennessee Supreme Court. By 1924, only nine tollgates were left in the county, including two on Nolensville Road that were owned by Johnson. In 1926, they all came down. Johnson argued in court for years about how much the county should pay him. In January 1928, Williamson County Commission voted to pay Johnson $60,000 for Nolensville, Franklin/Brentwood, and Franklin/Spring Hill Turnpikes. He was unsatisfied but acquiesced. (Both, courtesy of the Heritage Foundation.)

Sam Williams (1898–1963), son of J.W. Williams (1848–1940), sits in a horse and buggy in the 1800s. Williams married Louise Green and had two sons and one daughter born in Nolensville. (Courtesy of Carrie Stephenson Ozburn and Peggy Stephenson Wilson.)

Walter Layne and James M. Ragsdale conducted a mule-drawn streetcar in Nashville in the late 1800s. Ragsdale was a teacher in Hickman County before coming to Nashville, and an entry from his journal indicates that he began his job driving mule cars in the fall of 1887. Nolensvillian Tom Byrd was also a mule streetcar driver. (Courtesy of Marjorie Ragsdale Hernandez.)

A streetcar crew poses in Nashville about 1888. The man marked No. 1 is Walter Layne, and No. 2 is James M. Ragsdale. By 1918, at least 20 streetcar lines took passengers to numerous Nashville locations. Locally, Bargo Brittain ran a jitney, a taxi service that also carried mail between Nashville and Nolensville. (Courtesy of Marjorie Ragsdale Hernandez.)

Young LaUna Fly is shown here at about 16 years old. James Ragsdale picked her up in his streetcar along with another lady at Nashville's Maxwell House. On the ride, he asked her out for that night. He picked her up in a horse and buggy to attend a Christmas program at Hebron Methodist Church on Clovercroft Road. Soon married, James said that was the best streetcar pickup he ever made. (Courtesy of Marjorie Ragsdale Hernandez.)

Joseph John "J.J." Jenkins (1879–1967) sold country produce from a rig owned by S.G. Jenkins in the late 1800s. Old Puss, the horse in the photograph, helped Jenkins transport merchandise from Nashville to his general merchandise store in Nolensville. (Courtesy of Donald Jenkins.)

James (Jim) Allen "J.A." Williams (1874–1948) stands on the running board of his Federal truck, loaded with merchandise from his general store. The wheels are made of wooden spokes with solid tires. The general store was sold in 1930. The J.A. Williams building became the J.B. Ozburn granary and later the Puckett-Thomas grocery. (Courtesy of Larry Williams.)

James (Jim) Sherwood Jenkins (1908–1991) sits behind the steering wheel at his family home on Nolensville Road. The old car is considered to be a classic but can be envisioned in motion on Nolensville Road. (Courtesy of Donald Jenkins.)

A steam shovel is used to grade Nolensville Road in preparation for paving in the late 1920s to early 1930s in front of W.J. Putman's store. Just a few years earlier, tollgates had been taken down. For the first time, cars could drive to Nashville for free and on pavement. Nolensville children walked dirt roads to get to the pavement to roller skate down Nolensville Road. (Courtesy of Carrie Stephenson Ozburn.)

The advertisement on B.O. Williams's car reads: "B.O. Williams' General Store—Fresh meats and sandwiches." As with advertisements on wagons before them, marketing on automobiles promoted local businesses as they traveled Nolensville Road and beyond. (Courtesy of Larry Williams.)

This is another image of Nolensville Road looking toward town. In the early 1930s, a traveling circus passed through town on the road and caused quite a stir. Locals ran to the road to see two elephants being ridden and wagons with other animals headed south. (Courtesy of Carrie Stephenson Ozburn and Peggy Stephenson Wilson.)

The Stephenson children are shown in the 1940s as the family was preparing for a drive in the country. Many families limited driving trips during the turnpike era on Nolensville Road because of the expense of the tollgates. The community celebrated the end of that system and enjoyed the paved, barrier-free roadway from the 1930s on. (Courtesy of Carrie Stephenson Ozburn and Peggy Stephenson Wilson.)

A couple enjoys the mobility vehicles afforded in Nolensville. Willie Pearl Chrismon Jobe, who became the Ebenezer Church choir director, and Arthur Thomas Jobe relax and visit near the school on Rocky Fork Road. (Courtesy of Jackie McClain Green.)

Posing beside a car at Nolensville School in 1946 are, from left to right, (first row) Roberta May Green and Carolyn Hughes; (second row, standing) Patsy Gooch and Betty Lou Williams. Hughes was wearing her eighth-grade graduation dress. This was most likely taken on a Sunday afternoon, when ballgames were about to be played on the fields behind them. (Courtesy of Carolyn Hughes Battle.)

Hardie Williams (1914–1964) leans against his pickup truck in front of his brother's store in town. Williams was known to take his tractor and help drivers get over Nolensville Road's Tollgate Hill on snowy and icy days. (Courtesy of Peggy Williams Taylor and Kaye Williams Burns.)

James Howse Jr. (1943–2004) poses near his car. Howse served in the Army and comes from a longtime Nolensville family. (Courtesy of Jackie McClain Green.)

This 1951 photograph was taken 22 miles from Nashville on Nolensville Road. The landscape reveals the agrarian nature of the area prior to development. Trailways bus lines originating in Huntsville stopped in Nolensville en route to Nashville daily. Some Nolensville students took the Trailways bus to Nashville each day to attend high school in the 1940s and 1950s. (Courtesy of Metro Archives.)

Harry Graves Brittain (1898–1958) and Hortense Green Brittain ran this grocery store slightly north of the historic village across from Oldham Road. After Harry died in 1958, his brother Will, primarily a farmer, bought the store, which he operated with his wife, Polly Page Brittain. The detailed stone structure is noticeable to drivers traveling Nolensville Road and was crafted by Will Smith, brother of Cleo Smith Battle. (Courtesy of the Heritage Foundation.)

This McFarlin barn was on Nolensville Road near Burkitt Road and displayed painted advertising on its roof. It is recalled to have advertised "See Rock City" during the time before Interstate 65 and Interstate 24 were built. Nolensville Road would have been a main highway prior to the interstates between Nashville and Chattanooga, where Rock City is located. (Courtesy of Jim McFarlin.)

Five

CREAM AND THE CROPS

Nolensville's first settlers stayed in the area in part for its fertile soil. Deep into the 20th century, its rolling hills became a backdrop for hundreds of farms, which grew everything from corn and millet to tobacco. In addition to the land owners, tenant farmers worked the land.

The town became known for its dairy farms, which at one time may have numbered 50 or more. Dairying and farming are tough, 24-hour-day, seven-day-a-week businesses in which vacations are often not possible. Entrepreneurs to the core, a group of dairy farmers started a farmer-owned-and-operated creamery that was quickly profitable and sold thousands of pounds of butter from 1921 to 1957.

Other businesses popped up on farms, including a shoe repair shop, family-owned grocery stores, sawmills, and molasses mills. Residents lived off the land, growing their own gardens and their own meat. Children, who also worked on these farms, found fun in simple pleasures with pretend and real horses, dogs, outdoor toys, fishing ponds, and 4-H competitions, which might take them out of state to national competitions.

Children made up their own games, sometimes finding a little mischief along the way. One pair of girlfriends would set a purse with a string attached to it on the road and wait for a car to come. When the car stopped and the driver got out of the car, they would yank the empty purse as the driver was about to pick it up and run into the woods with a giggle. One local remembers his grandfather bragging about placing a wagon on a barn roof in the dark as a joke to be discovered the next morning.

At left, from left to right, Doug, Robert, and Sue Nichols come down from the barn after milking the cows in 1945. Everyone in the family worked, and milking was done every day at daybreak and late afternoon. Sometimes, they would set the pails in a spring to cool. Berry Douglas Nichols, then his son Herbert, and later Herbert's son Mark ran the dairy. The original home, at the corner of Kidd and Nolensville Roads, was most likely built between 1803 and 1806. Below, Lester Scales's dairy farm fronts Clovercroft Road. The lone building shown here, called Owens House, was the birthplace of Elton Scales in 1921. Four Scales brothers, P.E. "Buddy," J.T., Elton, and Lester, operated dairies on the road. (Left, courtesy of the Nichols family; below, courtesy of Phyllis Scales Sanford.)

These six-month-old calves still graze land that was originally a land grant to James Mulherin. It was divided, sold several times, and eventually bought by Benjamin Kidd and passed down to James Kidd, then William Kidd, who died in 1906. A Kidd operated a gristmill across the road on Mill Creek. Ben Hill McFarlin Sr. bought the Kidd homeplace in 1907 or 1909. His daughter Lena Sneathis McFarlin Nichols inherited it. Below, the Jenkins family ran a dairy farm and farmed tobacco at their property on Nolensville Road. Dairying is a constant business, with rare chances for vacations. Sometimes, the cows would get more attention than family, with 4:00 a.m. wakeup calls to milk and calving in the middle of the night. (Above, courtesy of Vicky Travis; below, courtesy of Donald Jenkins.)

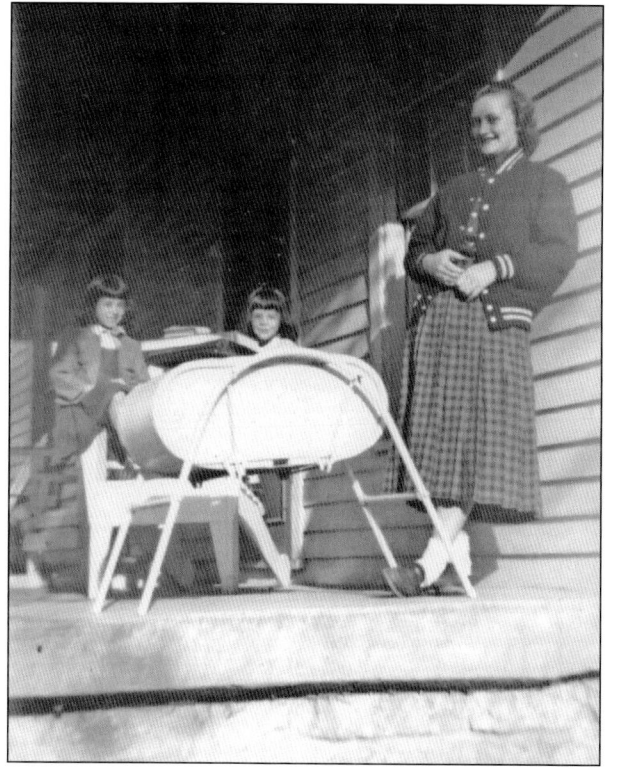

Betty Jenkins (Hughes) is pictured with nieces Pamela (left) and Sandra Jenkins churning butter on their front porch in Burke Hollow in 1952. (Courtesy of Betty Jenkins Hughes.)

Nolensville Co-Op Creamery churned butter in a 1,000-pound revolving drum in 1951. After about 30 minutes of churning, buttermilk was drained and the butter rinsed and salted; here, John Vernon takes it out to shape it into a 600-pound hunk to be chilled, then cut up. With no advertising, the good Jersey cow butter sold itself. A 1925 University of Tennessee Extension report counted two creameries in the county, the Nolensville Co-Op Creamery and a privately owned creamery in Franklin. Dairy farmers could sell their Grade A milk for consumption and their Grade B milk for butter and other dairy products. (Courtesy of the Vernon family.)

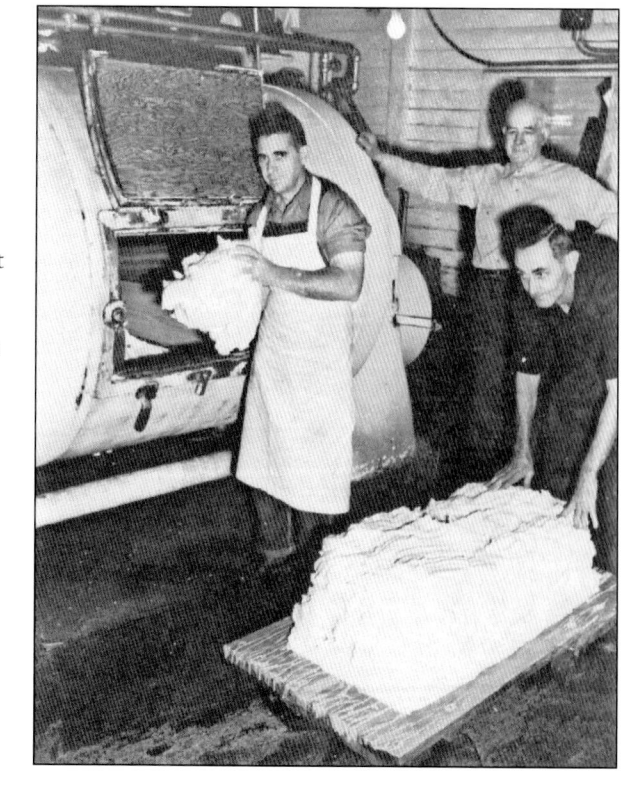

Roy D. Hughes watches his herd eat at his dairy farm on Rocky Fork Road in the late 1960s. During the Depression, it was very hard to make payments. When a banker came to foreclose in the 1930s, he saw the progress and how hard Roy was working and did not foreclose. The farm became very successful, and Roy was later named to the board of the Columbia branch of the Federal Land Bank, the same bank that had threatened foreclosure. At right, the Hughes farm was one of the first milk parlors with plate-glass windows. When cows came in, teats were on eye level, washed, and connected to electric milkers. It was kept immaculately clean, and milk never touched human hands. In the late 1960s and early 1970s, schoolkids would stop by to watch the activity in the parlor. (Both, courtesy of Carolyn Hughes Battle.)

At left, LaRue and Roy Hughes pose at the entrance to Silver Stream Farm on Rocky Fork Road in the summer of 1955. LaRue worked at the post office, so it is likely she was home for lunch. During World War II, German prisoners of war were bused to the farm to work in the fields. The prisoners would bathe in the creek before being returned to the prisoner of war camp south of Nolensville. After the farm and dairy were sold in the 2000s, the family asked that the farm name remain on the residential development. Below, Silver Stream Farm on Rocky Fork Road was named by LaRue Hughes, who loved a little sparkling creek that ran below the barn on the property. LaRue never threw away anything and worked with Roy to make the farm a success. From the early to mid-1900s, Nolensville was a hub for dairy farmers, at one time boasting about 50 dairies. (Both, courtesy of Carolyn Hughes Battle.)

Ben Hill McFarlin owned a breeding barn for jacks, without which there would be no mules. Before tractors, mules were the horsepower farmers needed. The farm bred "high-styled jacks," with "Starlight Jacks" a specialty. (Courtesy of the Nichols family.)

Emmett Jenkins is pictured on the Burke Hollow farm with a mule pulling the "slide" in the 1950s. Notice that the base looks more like a sled. The wooden runners kept the load under control on the hill better than wheels could. Farmers also used hillside, or turning, plows. While the tractor became the preferred way to work after World War II, a mule was still needed to haul on the hills and hollows. (Courtesy of Betty Jenkins Hughes.)

Elmer Sherwood Jenkins plows the garden with his son Jim, next to the horse, and relatives in 1918. Beginning in the late 1800s, Jenkins was a teacher and principal. With Elmer, everything was educational. Young family members learned about anatomy as he dressed a chicken and about fossils and rocks on a walk in the woods. (Courtesy of Donald Jenkins.)

Minus Cherry and Minus Jr. bale hay on their farm in the 1940s with the help of a mule team. In the late 1940s, many farmers made the shift to mechanically powered farming, which could increase productivity in an already tough occupation. The shift freed up land for farm use, as horses and mules needed year-round care and acres set aside for them. (Courtesy of Elaine Cherry Hughes.)

Wheat is threshed on the Jim Williams farm on land that later became Johnson Industrial Park and the Stonebrook subdivision. Hardie Williams operates the threshing machine as the wheat is hauled to it on wagons. Below, Lucien Battle drives the first tractor the Battle family was able to buy after World War II in 1949. Early on, very few farmers owned tractors. Tractors were rare on small farms in the 1920s and 1930s, and tractor design was being refined by manufacturers. In the cash-strapped Depression, buying a tractor was out of the question. After the war, when rationing was no longer required, sales of tractors jumped nationally. (Above, courtesy of Peggy Stephenson Wilson and Carrie Stephenson Ozburn; below, courtesy of Carolyn Hughes Battle.)

The Cherry family poses for a photograph. This was likely taken by a traveling photographer. It was not unusual for these photographers to stay with a family for a few days. From left to right are Josie Covington Cherry, sons Thomas and Minus Jr., and Minus. Josie is pregnant with Lottie. The family came to Nolensville in 1914, bought an 1860 home, and were active in Hebron Methodist Church on Clovercroft Road. (Courtesy of Elaine Cherry Hughes.)

Minus Cherry Jr. (right) cuts tobacco on the Cherry farm on Clovercroft Road. Tobacco was cut and left to dry in the field for a day until the leaves wilted, then it was hauled to hang in the barn to dry. (Courtesy of Elaine Cherry Hughes.)

Pete Burke (left) and Minus Cherry Jr. sit in the Cherry Farm barn on Clovercroft Road where tobacco was hung to dry. Tobacco farmers depended on cooperative weather and dealt with bugs like hornworms to bring in a good crop. Tobacco was one of Williamson County's cash crops along with millet and corn in the mid-1900s. (Courtesy of Elaine Cherry Hughes.)

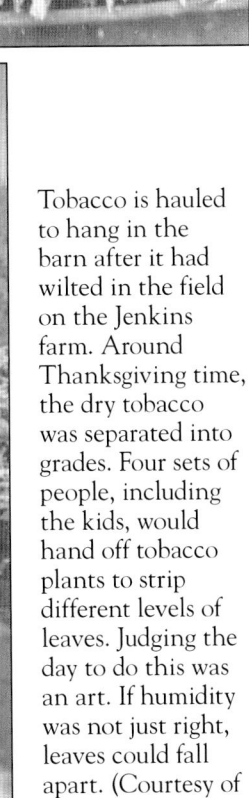

Tobacco is hauled to hang in the barn after it had wilted in the field on the Jenkins farm. Around Thanksgiving time, the dry tobacco was separated into grades. Four sets of people, including the kids, would hand off tobacco plants to strip different levels of leaves. Judging the day to do this was an art. If humidity was not just right, leaves could fall apart. (Courtesy of Donald Jenkins.)

From left to right, Hunter Battle, William Farrow "Buck" Chrismon, Searcy McClain (1913–2001), Lucien Battle (1931–2017), unidentified, and Bill Chrismon work to lift up a hog to weigh it. A homegrown, cornfed hog might weigh about 700 pounds. After it was shot between the eyes, weighed, and gutted, its large and small intestines were saved to prepare as chitlins. The hog would be boiled, its hair scraped off, and butchered. Hog killing was always done in cold weather in late November or early December. (Courtesy of Carolyn Hughes Battle.)

From left to right, unidentified, Bob Stephens, wife Mabel, unidentified, Fannie Gray, and Mae Lizzie Stephens pose in their scalding trough about 1928. Families would travel to use this trough during hog killing time as it was the only metal one in the Burke Hollow area. (Courtesy of Mae Lizzie Stephens Pulley.)

Murray Polk (left) and Searcy McClain make lard during the annual hog killing at Silver Stream Farm. After the hog was butchered, much fat was cut out, rendered in iron kettles, and stirred with boat oars. The liquefied fat was poured into aluminum cans to be stored as lard for cooking. The cracklins, little pieces of fried skin, were used to flavor cornbread, called "cracklin' bread." (Courtesy of Carolyn Hughes Battle.)

Children are shown on their farm on York Road. From left to right are (first row) George Lee Floyd, Annie Pearl Floyd, and Lillie Ruth Floyd; (second row) Leslie Felix Polk, John Ashley Floyd, and Frank Thomas Polk (1934–2012.) (Courtesy of Alfreda Polk Cotton.)

T.H. Guthrie of Nolensville cares for his litter of three-month-old pigs for a 4-H project. His litter was exhibited at the county fair and made a hit, according to a 1924 University of Tennessee Extension report. Of 11 members who signed up to compete, he was the only one who did the work, it said. He was able to sell some breeding stock after exhibiting them. (Courtesy of the University of Tennessee Extension Williamson County.)

Cleo Smith Battle (1893–1992) feeds sheep on the farm on Battle Road. In her younger days, she taught at the Split Log School in the 1910s. (Courtesy of Carolyn Hughes Battle.)

The Jackson sawmill, shown here in 1901, is believed to have been at the corner of Nolensville Road and Sunset Road, across from the Pleasant Valley Church of Christ (known as Mill Creek Church of Christ in 2018). Lumber from this mill was used in the construction of Mount Olivet Methodist Church in 1894, later renamed Nolensville First United Methodist Church. Below, Horace Williams (left) and Jack Stephenson work at a sawmill on the Williams property at the corner of Williams and Nolensville Roads. A sawmill was always a dangerous place; Horace's brother Percy died after a log hit him in the head. (Above, courtesy of the Heritage Foundation; below, courtesy of Peggy Williams Taylor and Kaye Williams Burns.)

Molasses mills are pictured here; the one below is identified as the Brittain molasses mill. Once an important source of sweetener, molasses was made from the sorghum cane grown prevalently on farms in the 1850s. Most farmers grew enough cane for their own use, while others treated it as a cash crop. Local vicinities had at least one farmer with a mill and evaporating pan. Neighboring farmers would bring their cane to be squeezed by the mule-powered mill and cooked into a syrup. The earliest mills were made of wood and crafted by an inventive farmer or a blacksmith. Local residents recall cutting the heads off the sorghum stalks before they were fed to the press. Some children sent to fetch water during school would get sidetracked to pick a sweet sorghum cane to chew on. When the juice was cooking, the sweet smell would linger. (Both, courtesy of the Heritage Foundation.)

The Holt lead mine off Sam Donald Road, shown in the early 1900s, was mined during World War I. Lead is found in East and Middle Tennessee, often in limestones and dolomites. The Tennessee Department of Environment and Conservation notes that the state has a history of mining more different kinds of minerals than any other east of the Mississippi River, with the exception of North Carolina. (Courtesy of TSLA.)

A **PUZZLING QUESTION.**

HOW CAN THE OLD BE MADE NEW?

HOLD THE PICTURE TO THE LIGHT, AND THE QUESTION IS ANSWERED.

With compliments of
Farmers' & Laborers' Co-operative Co.
Nolensville, Tenn.

GIES & CO. BUFFALO NY

This novelty card reads "Compliments of Farmers' & Laborers' Co-operative Co. Nolensville, Tenn." The card was possibly sponsored and distributed by its advertiser, Diamond Dyes. Advertising with trade cards like this was popular from the 1870s to 1900. The answer to the question "How can the old be made new?" is revealed when the card is held to the light: "Use Diamond Dyes. . . . It's easy to dye with Diamond Dyes. Anything. Any color." (Courtesy of the Tennessee State Museum.)

Doris Nichols and nephew Herbert Nichols stand on the porch of the McFarlin and Nichols store in the early 1940s at the corner of Kidd and Nolensville Roads. After war rationing was over, the store got red rubber balls. Little Herbert took one and got what he recalled as the "whupping of my life." The sign misspells McFarlin as "McFarland," but for reasons unknown, it stayed. The store's boards were later used to build a home in Burke Hollow. (Courtesy of the Nichols family.)

Civil War veteran, farmer, and trader Milton Harvey Stephens, shown here with his second wife, Mary Scruggs, in the 1910s, became Williamson County sheriff at age 73. His ancestors were early Nolensville area settlers. While transporting two men suspected of stealing on Kidd Road, he was shot in the back of the head on Wilson Pike near Split Log Road on June 27, 1919. One suspect was acquitted and the other convicted of voluntary manslaughter. (Courtesy of Betty Jenkins Hughes.)

Ben Chrismon (1877–1963) repaired shoes at his shop on Sunset Road. He and his brother Jim both worked there. The Chrismons created Sunset Park, which was used for decades by African Americans for Sunday afternoon ballgames, Fourth of July celebrations, and reunions. The left side of his store was used for concessions. In 1929, the park was the site for the Williamson County Colored Agricultural Exhibition. (Courtesy of Jessie Boyd Brown.)

The so-called "Goatman" and his son traveled from state to state and came through Nolensville for a number of years, sometimes camping in town. Residents remember other traveling salesmen, such as the Watkins man, who sold spices and vanilla that people could not get in stores. Photographers also traveled, lodging with a family while they took portraits. (Courtesy of the Nolensville Historic School.)

A McFarlin mother takes her boys on a pony ride. The baby colt might hold as much interest to the boys as the camera that took the photograph in the early 1900s. (Courtesy of Jim McFarlin.)

The house pictured was on lot No. 5 on the original plan of Nolensville, designed by Nolensville founder William Nolen in 1818. At the time the photograph was taken in July 1927, the home was owned by Billy O. and Marie Appleton Williams. (Courtesy of Larry Williams.)

At home on a Nolensville farm in the 1940s are, from left to right, (first row) Frank Polk (1934–2012), Leslie Polk, Charles Williams, and Thomas Williams; (second row) Thomas Howse, Lemon Morton, Clifton Jobe, Willie Polk, and Thomas Brown. (Courtesy of Alfreda Polk Cotton.)

The children in this early 1900s photograph on a wooden horse are believed to be Lena, Hortense, and Roberta McFarlin. The boy on the right is believed to be Ben McFarlin. They had real horses on their farm, so perhaps they were practicing their horse-riding skills. (Courtesy of Jim McFarlin.)

These finely dressed ladies reclining on the grass in the countryside are from the McFarlin family. The woman in the center is believed to be Pearl McFarlin, a beloved aunt who never married. (Courtesy of Jim McFarlin.)

From left to right, Adelaide Cochran, Elizabeth Jackson, Cleo Smith Battle, and Bob Battle Sr. sit on their porch on Battle Road. After moving to another home on Battle Road, Bob Battle Sr. died when son Bob Jr. was 16 and son Lucien was 13. Aunts Adelaide and Elizabeth helped care for them. The boys ran the dairy, waking up at 3:00 a.m. to milk cows and riding bikes to Nolensville Road to take a bus to Nashville's Central High School. (Courtesy of Carolyn Hughes Battle.)

Family members pose with family members at a Jones family gathering in the 1920s. From left to right are (first row) Steve Jones holding Mary, known as Tot, and Susie Jones holding Annie; (second row) Middy, Hattie, and Bennie. Steve Jones, the father of Dorothy Jones Polk, was born in 1929 after this photograph was taken. (Courtesy of Dorothy Jones Polk.)

William Stephens stands with granddaughters Margaret Louise Waters Smith and Evelyn Marie Waters Powell about 1925. Their homeplace was located on Molly Hollow Road in the Burke Hollow area of Nolensville. (Courtesy of Frankie Sullivan Shacklett.)

The homestead of T.C. Ozment on York Road is shown in 1942. The family lived on King Street for a time at a home that had an artesian well. Ozment installed a pump, and the well supplied water to King's Inn, the feed mill, a school, and a grocery store in town. Some neighbors would store their butter and cream in the well to keep it cool. (Courtesy of Amelia Ozment Hayes.)

After living in the family home for 70 years, Edward Green, youngest child of Sherwood Green (1766–1840), died in 1901 and left the home to his youngest child, Lundy Green (1873–1952), one of eight children. This photograph appears to be from a 1925 gathering. Outbuildings include an 1840 log kitchen and smokehouse and remnants of an 1840 slave cabin used as a milk house. It was listed in the National Register of Historic Places in 1988. (Courtesy of Janice Page Green.)

Annis Williams Ozburn (1911–1959) sits on the steps of their smokehouse on Osburn Road. Her father was store owner J.A. Williams. Known as strong-willed but sweet, she married J.B. Ozburn in 1929 and had two boys, Billy and Tommy. She helped start the 4-H fair in Nolensville, often driving kids and animals there and bringing chicken salad for lunch. (Courtesy of Carrie Stephenson Ozburn.)

Lucien Battle is on the porch of his Smith grandparents' home on Sunset Road. Notice the small chair under the table. It is still in the family's possession. (Courtesy of Carolyn Hughes Battle.)

From left to right, Allie Hicks Burke, Maggie Jenkins Burke, Dora Irvin Warren, and Sara Lenora (Nora) Burke Jenkins gather for lunch about 1953 at Emmett Jenkins's place on Burke Hollow Road. Ruth Jenkins liked to invite the neighbor ladies to lunch. (Courtesy of Betty J. Hughes.)

Thomas "Buddy" McClain (1884–1969) bought his farm on Sanford Road in 1918. He and his wife, Mary Delfield McClain, had seven children. Thomas's parents were Lewis McClarrin Jr. (1860–1936) and Sally Williams McClarrin (1866–1936). The surname McClarrin changed over the years to McClain. Thomas's grandfather Lewis McClarrin Sr. was a slave brought to Tennessee from Virginia. (Courtesy of Betty Williams Alzamora.)

Betty Williams (left) and Sarah Woods, around 12 years old, dressed up for a trip to Nashville and got their photograph taken at the Arcade. The girls, who lived on neighboring farms off Rocky Fork Road, would walk with their roller skates to get to the paved Nolensville Road to skate. Bored at a PTA meeting, the two once peeked into the boys' outhouse. They were tattled on and had to write "I will not look into the boys toilet" 100 times. (Courtesy of Betty Williams Alzamora.)

Bill (against the truck) and Bob Stephenson load leaves into the truck. Their mom, Ora Stephenson, liked the yard clean of leaves, so their job was to haul leaves to the woods. (Courtesy of Carrie Stephenson Ozburn and Peggy Stephenson Wilson.)

McFarlin children play on a post in the yard at the homeplace. The photograph is believed to be from between 1900 and 1910, with Roberta being the little girl standing beside the post. (Courtesy of Jim McFarlin.)

From left to right, Emmett Layne Jr., Bill Stephenson, Carrie Stephenson (Ozburn), and Peggy Stephenson (Wilson) play with a small cart. The goat, named Charlie, is positioned where the mule would be in a full-size cart. (Courtesy of Peggy Stephenson Wilson and Carrie Stephenson Ozburn.)

Above, Lucien Hunter Battle (left) plays in the cart with brother William Robert Battle Jr. and dog Sandy. Notice the wood frame of the house in the background. Below, a few years later, Lucien stands with a horse with sister Betty Lelia Battle Green on it and a pony at the same location. Will Smith, brother of Cleo Smith (Battle), who worked on the stone cottage that was Brittain's store on Nolensville Road, also crafted the stone work on this house. (Both, courtesy of Carolyn Hughes Battle.)

In July 1953, Pete Vernon and his son Earl stand on what would later be named Vernon Road. Barbara "Bobby" Vernon, mother of five and a letter carrier, recommended their rural route road be named for the family in the 1960s. The earliest Vernon to come to Nolensville was Capt. Richard Vernon, who served in the Revolutionary War. He came in 1825 during one of the North Carolina migrations. (Courtesy of Karon Vernon.)

Steve Jones (left) and Wiley Jobe walk to the porch in the late 1950s. Jones passed away in the early 1960s. Wiley Jobe, a blacksmith, married Cora Bell Page Jobe in 1912 and raised eight children. They bought 45 acres on Sanford Road and owned two mules, horses, cows, hogs, goats, sheep, and chickens and had a large garden. Wiley Jobe also "witched water" (found its location) for many wells in the area. (Courtesy of Dorothy Jones Polk.)

Larry Williams stands ready with his fishing pole to head out to the pond on the family's Clearview Farm at three years old in 1950. The land seen here, on the east side of Nolensville Road north of the historic district, was later sold and became the site of a church and a veterinary clinic. When Williams got older, he enjoyed working summers at Newt McCord's neighboring farm. Williams is a descendant of John William Williams (known as J.W. Williams, 1848–1940), who played an active role in the development of the town of Nolensville. Below, from left to right, fishing buddies Will Brittain, Randolph Williams, Teddy Williams, and Harry Brittain show off their catch after a trip to the Tennessee River near Jackson. (Both, courtesy of Larry Williams.)

Tennessee sent delegates to the third National 4-H Club Camp in 1927. Nolensville's James Guthrie (far left) represented Williamson County. Guthrie started competing in 1924, raising a pig that won first prize in the county fair. He raised a Jersey calf and corn, winning several additional first prizes. Twenty years later, a 1947 University of Tennessee Extension report shows that 4-H expanded enrollment to 36 clubs around the county, including Nolensville. (Courtesy of the University of Tennessee Extension Williamson County.)

Williamson County won second place in competition with 10 other counties at the 1924 state fair with a prize of $500. This image is not just about agriculture but also about a big issue of the day: the sign in front reads "The Tollgates Are Going." The county condemned tollgates, including those on Nolensville Road, and started buying out their owners in 1926. (Courtesy of the University of Tennessee Extension Williamson County.)

Six

COMING TOGETHER

Creative, strong, competitive people built Nolensville's churches, schools, and recreation areas. They worked hard, played hard, and prayed hard. A giving spirit has long been a thread that tied the community together. A 1900 *Nashville Tennessean* story tells of a storm that came through, sweeping away some homes and killing at least one community member: "The residents of Nolensville have responded nobly to every call made upon them. They have thrown open their houses to those in need of homes, given food and clothing without stint to the storm sufferers."

People came together within their families and social circles. An Odd Fellows lodge was dedicated in 1868 where the Masons also met. The Nolensville Club, formed in 1926, was dedicated to community service and educational homemaking demonstrations. Renamed the Friendly Neighbors in 1969, it was the force that created the Nolensville library with Williamson County. Since 1955, the Nolensville Lions Club has contributed to the community. In the early 1970s, the Nolensville Jaycees created the Nolensville Volunteer Fire Department.

Several saloons dotted Nolensville Road, which for several decades had quite an unsavory reputation, not unlike other rural roads in the county. One resident raised in a prominent family in Nashville was not permitted to come to Nolensville as a young lady. Through the efforts of a dedicated county sheriff and community muscle, Nolensville's reputation improved. Fun was also found in square dancing, home parties, roller skating, and sports. Kids and teens found a little mischief sometimes, smoking crossvine or racing cars on Nolensville Road.

In the mid-20th century, folks still felt like they knew everybody. Mirroring America at the time, blacks and whites were segregated at churches, schools, recreation areas, and even saloons. Entrances at some stores and restaurants in town were separate. Ben Chrismon built a park on his land so African Americans had a place to play ball and gather. A community group raised money during the Depression to build a much-needed school. While institutionally separated, black and white families would often help each other as well as work and play together. In the 1960s, this community would go on to have one of the most recognized school integration experiences in the nation.

In 1931, even the Depression did not stop more than 1,000 Williamson County children, including Nolensville's, from rallying and celebrating National Child Health Week in Franklin at an event that included a parade. Spring Hill's Branham-Hughes School band is seen in the public square in the center of the photograph at left. Below, Frank Byrd shows his calf at a dairy show. Since the 1920s, many Nolensville youth were involved in the University of Tennessee Extension's 4-H program, competing for top prizes in farming, home economics, and leadership. The Nolensville Community Club sponsored a junior 4-H show for more than 40 years. (Left, courtesy of the University of Tennessee Extension Williamson County; below, courtesy of the Nolensville Historic School.)

Marjorie Claire Hughes (1934–2018), left, and sister Carolyn Hughes show their calves Rose and Sweetie Face at a 4-H show in Franklin. Their grandfather David McDonald stands behind them. They also competed in the Nolensville show and the state fair, where the girls spent a week grooming, shampooing, and brushing their calves. Girls were not allowed to stay overnight, so they had to go back and forth each day, bringing ham and pimento cheese sandwiches. (Courtesy of Carolyn Hughes Battle.)

This Nolensville float in a Franklin parade during the 1940s features a cow and signs about the farming community: buttermilk, whole milk, soybeans, and more. Carolyn Hughes and David Gooch ride up front. While baseball and basketball were the main organized sports of the day, 4-H farm contests were popular among kids and teens. (Courtesy of the Nolensville Historic School.)

Founded as Mount Olivet Methodist Episcopal Church in 1837, the original log building was a few miles south on Williams Road with a dirt floor and split-log seats for 37 members. It was also a school. A second church building was damaged by Union and Confederate troops. In 1894, the church started building on Nolensville Road, shown here about 1918. (Courtesy of Archives of the Tennessee Conference United Methodist Church.)

Before Nolensville Road was paved in the late 1920s, a field was beyond the church, which had minimal support underneath. Much of the lumber for this church came from Jim Jackson's sawmill on Mill Creek, which is thought to have been across from the Church of Christ at Nolensville and Sunset Roads. (Courtesy of Carrie Stephenson Ozburn and Peggy Stephenson Wilson.)

A horse rider identified as Ben McFarlin rides up to the church, which went through several name changes over the years. When the Methodist Church split over the issue of slavery in 1844, Mount Olivet was renamed Mount Olivet Methodist Episcopal Church South. In 1939, the church conference dropped "Episcopal" and "South" and voted that all churches unify under the name "Methodist Church." That is when Mount Olivet became Nolensville Methodist Church. It became United Methodist in 1968. Eventually, the church was renamed Nolensville First United Methodist Church. Below, in 1943, a banner hangs at the front of the sanctuary listing those serving in World War II. In the 1930s, the church added a basement. Classrooms and offices were added in the 1950s and 1970s, and a fellowship hall and more were added in 2000. (Right, courtesy of Jim McFarlin; below, courtesy of Carolyn Hughes Battle.)

First known as Pleasant Valley Church, this frame building had one door for men and another for women and children. It still stands at the corner of Nolensville Road and Stonebrook Boulevard. The church was moved back 125 feet when Nolensville Road was paved, and a rock levee was built in the late 1920s. During storms in May 1984 and May 2010, the levee broke, and the church flooded. Other churches and neighbors helped repair it. (Courtesy of Mill Creek Church of Christ.)

In 1894, Pleasant Valley Church members gather in front of their new building, for which Thomas B. Newsom (far right) donated the land. The first records for this church show a gospel meeting held on July 19, 1891. Founding members included the Gooch, Kidd, Haley, Hall, and Brittain families. Name changes include Newsom Chapel, Christian Church of Nolensville, and Nolensville Church of Christ. (Courtesy of Mill Creek Church of Christ.)

On June 30, 1888, Hebron Methodist Episcopal Church on Clovercroft Road was dedicated. Nolensville Baptist bought the former Hebron Methodist building for $1,500 in 1952. In the following decades, Nolensville Baptist built Sunday school rooms, a vestibule, an awning, a porch, and a fellowship hall. With help from membership, the projects were debt free. A story goes that a preacher once gave a sermon from the roof. (Courtesy of Margie Scales Hartman.)

From left to right, Nannie Scales, Cherry Mitchell, and Patricia Mitchell leave church at Nolensville Baptist in 1961. Sunday school teacher Scales was nicknamed "Miss Cookie" because she brought homemade cookies every Sunday for the kids. The trees at left provided shade for dinner on the grounds, a tradition every June to start or end a revival. Before the church was established in 1951, tent revivals were held at farms. (Courtesy of Margie Scales Hartman.)

In the early 1960s, Nolensville Methodist Church was renamed Ebenezer Methodist Church. In 1968, after a merger of church bodies, it added "United" and was renamed Ebenezer United Methodist Church. Additions to the building on King Street have included a kitchen, restrooms, a baptismal pool, stained-glass windows, and an educational annex. Land on King Street was deeded to the African American community in 1869 with the stipulation that it be used for a church. Services began in an old farmhouse. In 1916, the county and the community built a two-story frame building to use as a church and a school. It was condemned in the early 1940s, and members built a new stone-block church around the frame building, which was then torn down from the inside. At left, from left to right are (first row) Frank T. Polk Jr. and Frezena Addrenia Polk; (second row) Beulah T. Polk and Leslie (Les) F. Polk holding Lillie Alfreda Polk at Ebenezer Church's homecoming in 1965. (Above, courtesy of the Heritage Foundation; left, courtesy of Alfreda Polk Cotton.)

At right, sisters Minnie Page Chrismon (left) and Cora Bell Page Jobe (1889–1974) visit after church around the 1950s. Minnie Chrismon was a midwife who delivered hundreds of babies, both black and white. Below, from left to right, Laura Holt Chrismon, Virginia Rucker, Ben Chrismon, Birdie Battle Chrismon, William Battle, Aggie Hyde Chrismon, and Paula Hyde celebrate. Before integration, Ben Chrismon built the 11-acre Sunset Park on his land on Sunset Road. The park became well known around the county and in Nashville as a place for African American families to gather for Sunday afternoon ballgames, picnics, and family reunions. (Right, courtesy of Jackie McClain Green; below, courtesy of the Heritage Foundation.)

Above, Frank Polk played with the Nolensville Stars at Sunset Park in the 1950s. A 1947 story in *The Nashville Tennessean* listed a Fourth of July event at the park sponsored by the Nolensville Baseball Club with a prize-winning game between the Nolensville Giants and the C.B. Ragland Club. At right, Woodrow Williams (1917–1990) played as a youth at Sunset Park and was recruited by the Negro National League. Shown at his barracks during World War II, Williams pitched for the Baltimore Elite Giants from about 1938 to 1940. A 1938 *Pittsburgh Courier* story credits Williams with holding the opponent to just two hits, winning the game. The left-handed pitcher was hit in the elbow with a line drive, ending his ball career. He served five years in the Army, married Katie Lee Jordan, and raised five children in Nolensville. (Above, courtesy of Alfreda Polk Cotton; right, courtesy of Marie Babb.)

Owner Ben Chrismon founded Sunset Park between 1909 and 1920, building ball fields, rock walls, and a small golf course. Along with food and ballgames on many a Sunday afternoon, events at the park included the Williamson County Colored Agricultural Exhibition in 1929. The Nolensville Stars, shown above in 1959, competed regionally. Chrismon, a shoe cobbler, had a shop that stood at the front of the park near Sunset Road. One side of it was used for concessions on Sundays. Chrismon died in 1963 at age 86. Tom and Jessie Brown bought the home and land in 1965 and continued to host games and reunions for about another decade. At right, Eugene and Pearl Chrismon Jobe are pictured near one of the rock walls Ben Chrismon built at Sunset Park. (Above, courtesy of the Nolensville Historic School; right, courtesy of Jackie McClain Green.)

Jim Turner, known as "Milkman Jim," was honored with a Jim Turner Day proclamation at Nashville's Sulphur Dell in April 1953. From left to right are an unidentified official, Gov. Frank Clement, Turner, New York Yankees manager Casey Stengel, and Nashville mayor Ben West. Married to Pauline Sanford, Turner spent 51 years in the major leagues as a pitcher for the Braves, Reds, and Yankees, becoming the Yankees pitching coach in 1948. In the offseason, he worked in his family's dairy business. He died in 1998 at the age of 95. (Courtesy of Metro Archives.)

Nolensville plays Franklin in the first game with lights in 1959. The Nolensville Community Center, organized in 1959, worked to get lights on ballfields behind Nolensville School. The momentous night of light capped a full day of kids' ballgames, pony rides, and a barbecue to celebrate the efforts of the Nolensville PTA, Nolensville Lions Club, and Middle Tennessee Electric Membership Corporation. (Courtesy of *Tennessee Magazine*.)

The baseball field directly behind the Nolensville Historic School was named for Jack Stephenson, who managed and coached a men's baseball team from the 1950s to 1970s. He maintained the ballfield, the grass, and the infield with his own tractor and equipment. A ceremony in 1989 honored him, and the field was dedicated in his name. Below, in 1973, Lanny McGowan stands to the right of one of many youth baseball teams he coached. The school can be seen directly behind them. For his years of commitment to coaching youth baseball, another ball field behind the school was named for McGowan. (Right, courtesy of Peggy Stephenson Wilson and Carrie Stephenson Ozburn; below, courtesy of Lanny and Lois McGowan.)

In the early 1900s, Nolensville School was off Clovercroft Road near the cemetery. A precursor to this school, which no longer exists, was Nolensville Academy, which burned in 1902. A March 8, 1902, *Nashville Tennessean* story said the cause was unknown. "The school was never in a more prosperous condition. There was a loss of $2,000, with no insurance." Nolensville Female Academy was incorporated in 1850 and was one of several such institutions around the county. (Courtesy of Donald Jenkins.)

Teacher Cleo Smith Battle watches her students play ring around the rosy at the Split Log School in 1913. The original school was built before 1850 of logs from Fly-Ragsdale land that were split by hand. It burned but was rebuilt as this one-room schoolhouse in 1888, and the final class was held here in 1948. Similar small schools, such as Central School, Williams School, Battle School, and Pleasant Hill School, dotted the rolling hills. (Courtesy of the Heritage Foundation.)

From 1943 until integration in 1966, African American students attended Nolensville School No. 2 on Rocky Fork Road and Newsome Lane, an area that would later become a county park. The school had a classroom for grades one through four, another for grades five through eight, a small library, a clothes closet, and a coal-burning stove. After integration, the building may have been used for storage. Decades later, fire destroyed it. (Courtesy of TSLA.)

Teachers Lucinda Rucker (left) and Gloria Maryland, seen behind the students in this 1947 photograph, each taught four grades: first to fourth and fifth to eighth. Maryland would later teach at the integrated Nolensville Elementary School. Students were sent every morning to get water for the day from a well near Newsome Lane. Some stopped to pick sorghum stalks or "rabbit ice," which is ice crystals on plants. (Courtesy of the Heritage Foundation of Williamson County.)

Nolensville

THIRD ANNUAL

Horse Show

SPONSORED BY NOLENSVILLE P. T. A.

SATURDAY, JUNE 27, 1936
AT 7:30 P. M.   NEW SCHOOL GROUNDS

Number of Prizes Classes and

CLASS NO 1 PONIES (under 34 inches) RIDERS UNDER 12 YEARS		$2.00	$2.00	.50
CLASS NO 2 WALKING HORSES (under 4 years)		$7.50	$5.00	$2.00
CLASS NO 3 COLT CLASS (under 2 years)		$3.00	$2.00	$1.00
CLASS NO 4 GAITED PONIES (50 inches and under)		$3.00	$2.00	$1.00
CLASS NO 5 MODEL CLASS (any age under halter)		$6.00	$3.00	$2.00
CLASS NO 6 WALKING PONIES (50 inches and under)		$5.00	$3.00	$1.00
CLASS NO 7 THREE GAITED MARE GELDING OR STALLION (any age)		Trophy	$5.00	$3.00
CLASS NO 8 WALKING MARE (any age)		$7.50	$5.00	$3.00
CLASS NO 9 ROADSTER CLASS		5.50	$5.00	$3.00
CLASS NO 10 WALKING HORSE GELDING OR STALLION		Trophy	$5.00	$3.00
CLASS NO 11 FIVE GAITED MARE GELDING OR STALLION		$3.00	$5.00	$3.00
CLASS NO 12 WALKING HORSE SWEEPSTAKE		$3.00	$5.00	$3.00
Trophy for the highest ranking horse in this class with a natural tail given by J. M. Dickerson, Travelers Rest Farm				
CLASS NO 13 JUMPING CLASS		5.00	$3.00	$1.00

No Entrance Fee For Livestock
Ring Will Be Well Lighted
Competent Judges, Loud Speakers, Music
NOT RESPONSIBLE FOR ANY ACCIDENTS
BARBECUE   HAMBURGERS   ICE CREAM   DRINKS
WILL BE SOLD BY P. T. A. FOR BENEFIT OF SCHOOL

ENTRIES FOR NAMES IN PROGRAM MUST BE ENTERED BY JUNE 25 TO MISS ELISE MAE PUCKETT SECRETARY
PHONE 56

Admission   10c 20c   Seats   15c   Parking   15c

NEWT. McCord. Mgr   A. A. HALL. Asst. Mgr.

Despite the Depression, the Nolensville community started raising money for a school with horse shows. The first horse show was put on in 1934, a tradition that would later be led by the Nolensville Lions Club and continued until 2008. History repeated itself in a way in 2009, when, during the recession, community members worked with the county and raised money to save the 1937 building, which became a museum. (Courtesy of Williamson County Public Library.)

School opened in the fall of 1937. After a new school was built in 1972, this building was later used as Nolensville's library, for youth sports, Scouts, church, and club meetings, and as a recreation and senior center. (Courtesy of the Nolensville Historic School and *The Tennessean*.)

A September 9, 1937, story in *The Nashville Tennessean* shows Pauline McArthur teaching in a tent because the new $12,000 school was not finished. With no such thing as air-conditioning, school in the tent was cooler that it might have been indoors. Boys were known to catch frogs and lizards and put them on top of the tent to shake down on girls. (Courtesy of the Nolensville Historic School and *The Tennessean*.)

After World War II, the Nolensville Community Club bought a war surplus building in Nashville, tore it down, and hauled it to the school to build a cafeteria and gymnasium. Other improvements that year included two school buses, shrubbery, fence painting, and an updated telephone system. The group also sponsored a 4-H calf show. The gym can be seen in the 1975 movie *W.W. and the Dixie Dancekings*, starring Burt Reynolds. A few locals, such as Jackie Hicklen Lawson, were lucky enough to be extras in the movie. (Courtesy of the Nolensville Historic School.)

Teacher Amelia Osburn poses with the third- and fourth-graders on the steps of Nolensville School in 1954. By 1950, the gym, indoor bathrooms, and kitchen had been completed at Nolensville Elementary School. The school was closed in 2009 for safety concerns by the county, but members of the Nolensville Historical Society researched and applied for National Register of Historic Places status, which was granted in 2012. Nolensville School used Julius Rosenwald building plans and is one of few such buildings in Williamson County. The Nolensville Historical Society renovated the building into a museum and event venue in cooperation with Williamson County. (Above, courtesy of Nolensville Historic School; below, courtesy of TSLA.)

Every morning at 9:00 a.m., two flags were raised at Nolensville School: the American flag and the 4-H flag. Many students from farm-centered Nolensville participated in 4-H clubs and contests. In the 1990s, a monument with a stone base was added to another flag pole near the building to honor local veterans. (Courtesy of the Nolensville Historic School.)

Pauline McArthur teaches first graders in 1955 in Nolensville School. McArthur is remembered as being quite strict. She taught for decades and was honored in 1954 by the community. She is also remembered for organizing many student performances, such as Tom Thumb weddings, piano and singing recitals, plays, and more. (Courtesy of the Nolensville Historic School.)

In March 1967, about 50 Nolensville students were brought to see Pres. Lyndon and Lady Bird Johnson during Columbia State College's dedication. Because of the ease with which Nolensville integrated its school, the Johnsons presented encyclopedia sets to Nolensville principal Raymond Robertson and students Gary Pope and Ken Warren. On the day of integration in 1966, grandfathers, both black and white, gathered at the school to ensure no one from outside town disturbed the peace. Children who played together now went to school together. Below, in the spring of 1972, Larry Williams stands behind his seventh-graders during the last year in this building. A new school would open next door that fall. Growth brought another new school in 2007, and the 1972 building was renovated into a county recreation center in 2015. (Left, courtesy of TSLA; below, courtesy of Larry Williams.)

BIBLIOGRAPHY

Bowman, Virginia McDaniel. *Historic Williamson County: Old Homes and Sites.* Franklin, TN: Territorial Press, 1971. Republished in 1989 by Sovran Bank.

Crutchfield, James and Robert Holladay. *Franklin: Tennessee's Handsomest Town: A Bicentennial History, 1799–1999.* Franklin, TN: Providence House Publishers, 1999.

The History of Tennessee Illustrated. Chicago, IL: The Goodspeed Publishing Co., 1886.

Little, T. Vance. *Gently Flows the Harpeth.* Nashville, TN: Panacea Press, 2009.

———. *Historic Nolensville Cemetery.* Brentwood, TN: Nolensville Cemetery Association, 1998.

Marsh, Helen C. and Timothy Richard Marsh. *Land Deed Genealogy of Davidson County 1797–1803.* Volume 3. Greenville, SC: Southern Hills Press, 1992.

Morrow, Sarah S. *The Legacy of Fannie Battle.* Nashville, TN: Fannie Battle Social Workers, 1980.

Nolensville Historical Society, Marie Batey, ed. *Nolensville Historical Society Journal 1–6.* Nolensville, TN: Nolensville Historical Society, 2005–2010.

Plattsmier, Elizabeth Burke. *The Families of Burke, Lamb, Jenkins, Naron.* Franklin, TN: 1991.

Smotherman, Carolyn, ed. History & Genealogy Group Fifty Forward, College Grove. *College Grove Williamson County, Tennessee, History and Families.* Nashville, TN: Panacea Press, 2011.

Van West, Carroll. *Tennessee Encyclopedia of History and Culture.* Nashville, TN: Rutledge Hill Press and the Tennessee Historical Society, 2002.

Warwick, Rick. *Williamson County in Black and White.* Franklin, TN: Williamson County Historical Society, 2000.

———. *Williamson County Civil War Veterans: Their Reunions & Photographs.* Nashville, TN: Panacea Press, 2007.

Warwick, Rick, ed. *Journal 30.* Williamson County Historical Society, 1999.

Wilson, Peggy Stephenson. *Nolensville 1797–1987: Reflections of a Tennessee Town.* Nashville, TN: Nolensville Recreation Center, Inc. Ambrose Printing Company, 1989.

INTERVIEWS:
Betty Williams Alzamora, Marie Babb, Carolyn Hughes Battle, Thelma Battle, Alfred Bennett, Evelyn Gillespie Hyde Bennett, Christine McFarlin Bess, Juanita Brown, Jessie Boyd Brown, Kaye Williams Burns, Dianne Calahan, Alfreda Polk Cotton, Jackie McClain Green, Janice Page Green, Margie Scales Hartman, Annabeth Hayes, Bob and Amelia Ozment Hayes, Marjorie Ragsdale Hernandez, A.B. (Johnny) and Sarah Woods Hicklen, Larry Hicklen, Betty Jenkins Hughes, Cheryl Hughes, Presley and Elaine Cherry Hughes, Donald and Virginia Jenkins, Sandra Johnson, Valerie Battle Kienzle, Bobby Land, Jackie Hicklen Lawson, Mildred Williams McCabe, Jim McFarlin, Sara Miller, Sam Miller, Pete and Bette Mosley, Herbert and Agnes Nichols, Mark and Sandra Nichols, Carrie Stephenson Ozburn, Jerry Patton, Elizabeth Burke Plattsmier, Dorothy Jones Polk, Mamie Polk, Kenneth and Phyllis Scales Sanford, Rosemary Smith, Peggy Williams Taylor, Karon Vernon, Nelda Burke Vest, Nick Waggoner, Larry Williams, Peggy Stephenson Wilson, Scott York, Larry York.

Discover Thousands of Local History Books Featuring Millions of Vintage Images

Arcadia Publishing, the leading local history publisher in the United States, is committed to making history accessible and meaningful through publishing books that celebrate and preserve the heritage of America's people and places.

Find more books like this at
www.arcadiapublishing.com

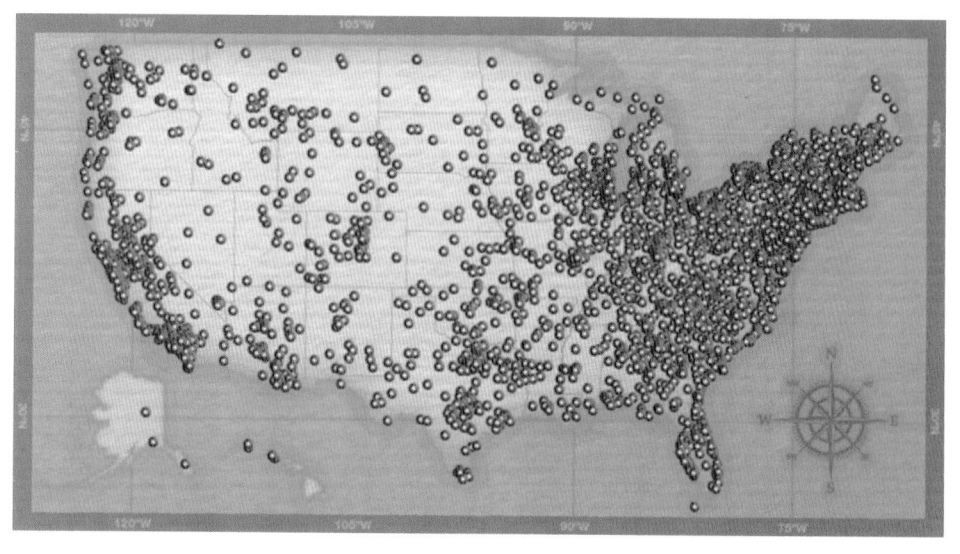

Search for your hometown history, your old stomping grounds, and even your favorite sports team.

Consistent with our mission to preserve history on a local level, this book was printed in South Carolina on American-made paper and manufactured entirely in the United States. Products carrying the accredited Forest Stewardship Council (FSC) label are printed on 100 percent FSC-certified paper.

MADE IN THE